The Literary Development of
John 13–17

SOCIETY
OF BIBLICAL
LITERATURE

DISSERTATION SERIES
Saul M. Olyan, Old Testament Editor
Mark Allan Powell, New Testament Editor

Number 182
THE LITERARY DEVELOPMENT OF
JOHN 13–17
A Chiastic Reading

by
Wayne Brouwer

Wayne Brouwer

THE LITERARY DEVELOPMENT OF JOHN 13–17
A Chiastic Reading

Society of Biblical Literature
Atlanta

THE LITERARY DEVELOPMENT OF JOHN 13–17

A Chiastic Reading

by
Wayne Brouwer
Ph.D., McMaster University, 1999
Adele Reinhartz, Dissertation Advisor

Library of Congress Cataloging-in-Publication Data

Brouwer, Wayne, 1954–
    The literary development of John 13–17: a chiastic reading / Wayne Brouwer.
        p. cm. — (Society of Biblical Literature dissertation series ; no. 182)
    Originally presented as the author's thesis (Ph.D.)—McMaster University, 1999.
    Includes bibliographical references.
    ISBN 0-88414-038-5 (alk. paper)
    1. Bible. N.T. John XIII–XVII—Language, style. 2. Chiasmus. I. Title.
    II. Dissertation Series (Society of Biblical Literature) ; no. 182.

BS2615.55 .B76 2001
226.5'066—dc21   00-052635

07 06 05 04 03 02 01 00   5 4 3 2 1

Printed in the United States of America
on acid-free paper

TABLE OF CONTENTS

CHAPTER 1

INTRODUCTION

Backing into a Good Notion

My first inclination toward a chiastic reading of the farewell discourse in the Fourth Gospel arose out of investigations that began in 1986. While teaching New Testament courses at the Reformed Theological College of Nigeria, in Mkar, I was confronted with the need to bring clarity and cohesion to my explanation of the structure and argumentation of John 13–17.

This proved to be far more difficult than I had anticipated initially. Although the vocabulary of the Fourth Gospel is relatively simple, and most of the extended passages within the book flow with little interruption, the farewell discourse taken as a whole has a number of cumbersome elements. For one thing, it appears to weave several themes back and forth in a manner that challenges linear readings, either inductive or deductive in logical development.

Moreover, it is obvious to any first time reader that there appear to be a number of "miscues" and disjunctures in the text. How could Jesus say so forthrightly, "But now I am going to him who sent me; yet none of you asks me, 'Where are you going?'" (16:5), when both Peter and Thomas had both just asked him that very question (13:36; 14:5), almost in exactly the same words? Why all the repetition of terms, phrases, and ideas from things spoken just shortly before this in chapter 14? And what theme or cohesive exhortation stretches throughout to pull together the seeming fragments of what often appears to be a meandering soliloquy?

It was in rereading the farewell discourse in its entirety, a number of times over, that certain keys to interpretation seemed to emerge as tangible precipitate. First, the repetition of words and themes seems balanced, and, in a way, perhaps even contrived. There are a number of times when a careful reader of John 13–17 catches herself or himself saying, "Wait! Did not Jesus say that same thing only a few lines back? Are we not returning down the same literary path we just travelled moments ago?" Even so, these repetitions do not have a random feel about them. They recur in stages, with a kind of measured intent.

Second, there appeared to be a kind of enveloping expression of Jesus' care in the foot-washing episode that introduces the discourse and in the prayer for divine protection with which the discourse concludes. Further, the discourse materials in between these limits seemed to move from the darkness of betrayal[1] in 13:36–38 up through promises of comfort and encouragement to a testimony of intimacy, before returning down a similar path to another brief expression of the gloom when Jesus foretells the disciples' fickle betrayal (16:29–33).

In other words, the repetitious discourse seemed to have purposeful movement, even if, from some points of view, this progress resembled reflexive gyrations that failed to conform to a linear explication of a theme in syllogistic fashion.

It was my perception of this sense of seemingly purposeful repetition that ultimately brought to mind the literary movements of chiastic storytelling that are scattered throughout the Hebrew Bible.[2] There appeared to be some similar repetitions and reflexive use of themes in the farewell discourse.

The Art of Chiasm

Broadly defined, chiasm is the use of a balance of words, phrases, or themes around a pivotal center idea, provided that the order of these words, phrases, or themes is inverted in the second half over

---

[1] Note the Evangelist's nocturnal reference in 13:30 at Judas' departure ("And it was night"). Similar expressions using themes of light and darkness are found in several places in the Fourth Gospel. Most pronounced is the coming of Nicodemus to Jesus in 3:1–2 "by night," and entering a conversation that ultimately finds its way "to the light" (3:21).

[2] It was during my initial years of graduate study at Calvin Theological Seminary in Grand Rapids, Michigan, that I first learned about chiasm in the Hebrew Bible from Professor John Stek. I will always be grateful for his keen insights and wise deliberation in reflecting on the texts of scripture. I hope that my suggestions here will stimulate thinking in others as his encouragement nurtured it in me.

against the ordering of the first half. The term "chiasm"[3] comes from a symbolic representation of the flow of word or theme order in such a passage diagrammed visually by plotting the parallel sections at the extremes of the twenty-second letter of the Greek alphabet. Chiasm is thought patterns developed in the fashion of the extremes of the Greek letter "chi" (X) rotating around the pivotal center crossing. Chiasm, as an expression of balanced ideas, is commonly found in children's rhymes, as in the following tongue-twisting pair of stanzas:

Peter Piper picked   a peck of pickled peppers.

A peck of pickled peppers   Peter Piper picked.

If Peter Piper picked   a peck of pickled peppers,

where's the peck of pickled peppers   Peter Piper picked?

In each couplet the last half mirrors the first half with a reverse ordering of the linguistic elements. It is because of this movement of the text that the key words in defining chiasm are parallelism, symmetry and inversion.

One of the most tightly focused of all definitions of chiasm is that given by Norrman. He calls chiasm "the use of bilateral symmetry about a central axis."[4] In other words, a single term or theme or a grouping of these is reflected in parallel units across the pivotal midpoint of a literary pericope. Although Norrman's analysis is focused on literature outside of the Hebrew scriptures or the New Testament, his definition is universally applicable.

---

[3] Or "chiasmus," as it is also called.

[4] R. Norrman, *Samuel Butler and the Meaning of Chiasmus* (London: St. Martin's Press, 1986), 276.

Thomson, for instance, begins with Norrman's terminology when he looks for chiasm throughout the New Testament.[5] At the same time, Thomson believes that it is necessary to give further elaboration regarding the character of the central axis upon which the chiasm is hinged. Norrman's definition, in its terseness, does not make clear whether the central axis is a unique statement in the text, or if it is merely a transitional break between two parallel elements. Since Thomson believes that either possibility is legitimate in the expression of chiasm, his more precise definition includes both options. He says that "chiasmus may be said to be present in a passage if the text exhibits bilateral symmetry of four or more elements about a central axis, which may itself lie between two elements, or be a unique central element, the symmetry consisting of any combination of verbal, grammatical or syntactical elements, or, indeed, of ideas and concepts in a given pattern."[6]

In Thomson's definition chiasm requires at least four phrases or literary elements clearly related to one another. His reason is clear: if there are only two symmetric phrases in a pericope, the result is simple parallelism. There is no way to know if a reflexive movement of thought happens between the parallel ideas. The latter merely restates the former. For example, using elements of the children's verse explored above, one might rewrite it in the following manner, retaining the parallelism, but losing the chiasm:

Peter Piper picked a peck of pickled peppers.
Peter Piper gathered a gross of green goodies.

In this rewriting of the verse there is once again parallelism between the first and second lines. Now, however, it is based upon the lines in their entireties restating the same information, only using different terms. There is no reflexive movement of thought, since no inversion of terms or elements remains. For that reason chiasm is not

---

[5] Ian H. Thomson, *Chiasmus in the Pauline Letters* (Sheffield: Sheffield Academic Press, 1995), 25.

[6] Ibid., 25–26. Thomson sets his position over against that of those who, like Breck, require a visible central axis in any expression of chiasm. Cf. John Breck, *The Shape of Biblical Language* (Crestwood, New York: St. Vladimir's Seminary Press, 1994), 33–35. For Thomson, the axis around which a chiastically-developed passage might revolve could be a non-paralleled central element, a paralleled pair of central elements, or the break between two central paralleled elements.

present: the second line merely restates the meaning of the first using words that have a similar meaning.

Similarly, if there are three phrases in a pericope, with the first and the third in symmetric parallelism, the whole literary unit is not necessarily a chiasm. Chiasm occurs only when there is a movement away from and then back to the parallel words or phrases. Thus, chiasm can only happen when at least two or more elements of a literary unit fall on either side of a center, and express similar content in a reflexive manner. If we take the example of Peter Piper once again, and expand upon it to include a third and central element in the following manner, there is still a mirroring relationship between the first and third lines:

> *Peter Piper picked a peck of pickled peppers.*
> *He brought them to the market.*
> *Peter Piper picked another peck of peppers.*

In this version of the tale, while the first and third lines are moderately parallel, they do not provide reflexive movement. They describe the same movement or idea, without leading the thought process along a particular path or its reverse. It is the reflexive mirroring—left to right, right to left; up to down, down to up; in to out, out to in—or other similar movements, that are required in order to express chiastic thought.

For that reason, according to Thomson, chiasm is present only where there are at least two specific phrases or ideas or literary movements on either side of a midpoint that make a reflexive journey over against their parallel counterparts on the opposite side of that axis.

While all agree with Thomson on this minimal requirement for assessing chiastic development, there are different perspectives regarding the character of the axis or centring element itself. For Thomson the centring element of a chiastically developed pericope may be either a unique, unparalleled phrase, or merely the literary break between two sets of reflexively paralleled phrases.[7] For most, however, a unique, unparalleled central element of the pericope must be present in order for chiasm to occur.[8] In fact, the prominence and

---

[7] Thomson, *Chiasmus*, 25–26.

[8] Cf. Nils Lund, *Chiasmus in the New Testament: A Study in the Form and Function of Chiastic Structures* (Peabody, Massachusetts: Hendrickson Publishers, 1992), 40–41.

axis character of the central element of a passage has long served as one of the clues to identifying chiasm development.

Indeed, it is the unique role of the vine and branches teaching of John 15:1–17 in the Johannine farewell discourse, surrounded as it is by repetitions of words, phrases and similar ideas, that has intrigued scholars and suggested to more than several that chiastic development may be at work in a large scale in the passage as a whole. This reflexive movement of parallel ideas and phrases initially drew me to a chiastic reading of the elements of John 13–17. Many words, phrases, and ideas are repeated throughout the discourse, as is evident even at a cursory reading. What becomes increasingly striking is the seemingly careful positioning of the repetitions, and the mirror-like inversions that take place between parallel themes as the discourse unfolds.

Still, there is a great difference between the simple reflexivity that might be found in several lines of poetry and the extended narrative of the Johannine farewell discourse. Thomson, in fact, as we shall see, would not even allow one to consider five chapters of biblical text as holding the possibility of chiastic development. Thus we shall have to probe more deliberately into the character of chiasm, and the viability of investigating what is sometimes called "macro-chiasm" in distinction from the "micro-chiasm" defined above. To this end we will need to look at some possible origins of chiasm and the manner in which it functions in storytelling and narrative development. Further, we will seek tools of measurement by which macro-chiasms may be assessed.

A Lingering Challenge

My early and somewhat naïve reading of the farewell discourse travelled with me through the years, and the interpretive questions it raised demanded further investigation. In my Master's level project for McMaster University I analyzed the exegetical data that were used by various interpreters to give a coherent frame to John 13–17. At that time I suggested that the divergence in approach and interpretation between those who relied heavily on historical critical tools and those who attempted a psychological[9] reading of the text might be overcome through a non-linear reading of the passage. Rather than assuming that meaning would come in the reading of the text as a series of sequential ideas (a linear reading), linked by editorial redaction[10] or mystical stair-climbing,[11] I offered the proposal that the discourse might be read with more profit as an example of "macro-chiasm,"[12] in which the various sections of a literary unit parallel one another in pairs across the mid-section of the passage. Since chiasm develops parallel ideas paired across a mid-section that is uniquely highlighted in significance for the larger passage, there is an ebb and flow of meaning that does not follow a direct linear path from beginning to end. When read as a chiasm, elements of the discourse that appear to be repetitious and non-sequential find a new association.

In the concluding section of my Master's project I suggested that a chiastic reading of the farewell discourse might address the concerns of both the diachronic and synchronic approaches to interpretation, providing an alternative perspective by which to allow these chapters to cohere as they stand in a meaningful way. "Diachronic" means "through time." Diachronic approaches account for the composite character of the discourses by suggesting accretions wedded together over a period of years. Reading the discourses in this way one need not find linear coherence in the text from beginning to end, since the text is

---

[9] That is, a reading which explains the interruptions or abrupt changes in the text as clues to psychological developments either in the mind of Jesus, as Fernando Segovia (*The Farewell of the Word* [Minneapolis: Fortress, 1991], 116–117) would have it, or in the nature of the spiritual plateau that is being attained by the disciples as they listen to Jesus' words, as Thomas L. Brodie (*The Gospel according to John* [New York: Oxford, 1993], 470–471) sees it.

[10] E.g., the perspective put forward by John Painter (*The Quest for the Messiah: The History, Literature and Theology of the Johannine Community*, 2nd edition [Nashville: Abingdon, 1993], 417–435), in which the various sections of the Farewell Discourse build upon previous versions of the discourse, and each new version forms a revised theological response to the changing ecclesiastical situation in which the community finds itself.

[11] E.g., the view elucidated by Brodie (*Gospel*, 427–440), which sees the successive sections of the discourse as depicting new plateaus of spiritual insight on an upward journey of faith.

[12] That is, chiastic literary movement on a scale larger than 5–10 lines of reflexive poetry, or a briefly told tale complete in several sentences. Dahood ("Chiasmus" in *International Dictionary of the Bible Supplement*, edited by K. Crim, [Nashville: Abingdon, 1976], 145) uses the terms "micro-chiasm" and "macro-chiasm" to denote the difference in chiastic reflexivity in passages of shorter or greater length.

seen as a redacted product of various sources, each with unique historical and literary dimensions. "Synchronic," on the other hand, means "at the same time." Synchronic approaches espouse the idea that the entire discourse is to be read as a continuous monologue/dialogue communicating meaning as a unit without reference to redactional development.[13]

Now, with much more investigation behind me, this study is a detailed attempt to address both the possibilities and the limitations of my early hypothesis regarding the best way to read the Johannine farewell discourse. As I noted in my earlier study, the diachronic interpretations of John 13–17 correctly deduce the composite nature of the discourse as it exists in its present form. Unfortunately, in an attempt to recover the original shape or character of the separate discourse units, these interpretations usually fail to find cohesion and meaning in the discourse in its present form.

At the same time, in their desire to find meaning and cohesion in the given form of John 13–17, synchronic interpreters usually understate the significance of repetitive elements, and attempt to load interruptive statements that linger from editorial redaction[14] with additional meaning that stretches the implications of Jesus' words in often unusual and highly speculative directions.

Several scholars have offered chiastic readings of the Johannine farewell discourse. Some of these will be reviewed in more detail further along in this study. Generally these chiastic readings of John 13–17 are an expression of synchronic interpretations, since they analyse the literary movements of the passage without reference to historical developments of the text.

The unique approach taken in this study is that of reviewing the historical-critical diachronic investigations in order to gain an understanding of the nature and grouping of the various literary sections, and then proposing a chiastic reading of these sections which affirms the coherence of the received text, as synchronic readers desire. This approach, then, begins to "combine" the strengths of both diachronic and synchronic analyses of the Johannine farewell discourse in a manner keenly desired by Ashton.[15]

---

[13] Cf. John Ashton, *Studying John: Approaches to the Fourth Gospel* (Oxford: Clarendon Press, 1994), 140–148, for a fuller treatment of these terms.

[14] Such as Jesus' command to arise and go in 14:31.

[15] Ashton, *Studying John*, 208.

Thesis Summary and Approach

Briefly stated, my thesis is this: although it is very difficult to read the mind of the Evangelist, or the redactor who brought elements of previously written material into the shape of the gospel as we have it today, it appears that the repetitive and reflexive elements of the Johannine farewell discourse fit together in a large chiasm bounded by expressions of spiritual intimacy with God on either end (the footwashing episode of chapter 13 and the prayer of chapter 17), and channelled toward the challenge to "abide" in Jesus at the center (15:1–17). In outline it could be diagrammed as follows:

A. Gathering scene (Focus on unity with Jesus expressed in mutual
love) 13:1–35

B. Prediction of the disciple's denial 13:36–38

C. Jesus' departure tempered by assurance of the
father's power 14:1–14

D. The promise of the παράκλητος ("Advocate")
14:15–26

E. Troubling encounter with the world
14:27–31

F. The vine and branches teaching
(*"Abide in me!"*)
producing a community of mutual
love 15:1–17

E₁. Troubling encounter with the world
15:18–16:4a

D₁. The promise of the παράκλητος ("Advocate")
16:4b–15

C₁. Jesus' departure tempered by assurance of the
father's power 16:16–28

B₁. Prediction of the disciples' denial   16:29–33

A₁. Departing prayer (Focus on unity with Jesus expressed in mutual
                                                love)   17:1–26

Read in this manner John 13–17 takes on a different character than it would if understood primarily as a linear discourse. For one thing, the Vine and Branches teaching of 15:1–17 becomes the apex of its development, proclaiming the dominant theme that spiritual unity with Jesus (summarised a number of times in the phrase "abide in me") is at the center of the discourse, shaping and pervading the surrounding material. Also, the repetitive themes of betrayal, Jesus' leaving, the promise of the spirit as "Advocate," and the character of the disciples' interaction with the world, initially stated in chapters 13 and 14, become paired in a meaningful way with their counterparts in chapters 15 and 16. Each of these themes becomes an extension of the "Abide in me!" injunction of 15:1–17, explicating its significance in one of several ways.

Finally, there is, in this chiastic reading of the discourse, an understanding of the footwashing scene, which serves as a prelude to the discourse proper (13:1–35), as being a counterpart to the prayer of chapter 17. If union with Jesus is the organising theme of the discourse, the disciples enter the discourse through a visible expression of Jesus' desire for their intimacy, and leave with a spiritual expression of that same desire.

Although this reading of John 13–17 is similar in various elements to other chiastic proposals, several of which will be explored more fully, it is rooted in the dual assumption that both the historical development of the text and its current form are of significance for interpretation. As a result it serves to provide a cohesive understanding of the text in its received shape (which is the goal of synchronic interpreters) while at the same time encouraging the investigations of historical criticism to provide insight into the redactional development of the literary panels of the discourse (the emphasis of diachronic interpreters). In this manner, reading the farewell discourse chiastically brings resolution to many of the issues of interpretation that have stood between the diachronic and synchronic approaches. Allow me to summarise these briefly.

Diachronic Perspectives

Among those who hold to a "rough" reading of the farewell discourse in the Fourth Gospel, there are two major perspectives. First of all, following the lead of Bernard and Bultmann, some claim that the discourse has lost its original pagination, and is in need of some rearrangement of sections before it will make sense. Bernard was the first to develop a comprehensive restructuring of the farewell discourse. Like others before him, Bernard was aware of the awkwardness at several points in John 13-17. He argued that, in an early edition of the gospel, some pages of the text had been shuffled inadvertently.[16] This is not altogether unknown among ancient manuscripts.[17] Bernard calculated the average number of letters per page of typical manuscripts, and determined that approximately every 750 characters a new leaf would be needed. He blocked off the chapters of the farewell discourse into appropriately sized units and rearranged these units in a way that seemed to provide a better literary flow. His version of the "original" Johannine farewell discourse looked like this:[18]

- 13:1–31a—*The Last Supper: Feetwashing and Betrayal.*
- 15:1–16:33, 13:31b–13:38, 14:1–14:31—*The Discourse Proper.*
- 17:1–26—*The Prayer of Jesus.*

Bultmann later aligned himself with the assumptions underlying Bernard's hypothesis, and developed a similar repositioning of elements of the farewell discourse. One significant difference, however, was his positioning of the prayer in chapter 17. While Bernard believed that it functioned best to conclude the discourse as a whole,[19] Bultmann thought that it actually replaced the last supper sacramentalism that is so curiously missing from the Fourth Gospel.[20]

---

[16] J. H. Bernard, *The Gospel According to St. John,* International Critical Commentary (Edinburgh: T & T Clark, 1928), xvi–xxx.

[17] Cf. Rudolf Schnackenburg, *The Gospel According to St John,* Vol. 1 (New York: Crossroad, 1987), 53–54.

[18] Bernard, *Gospel,* 453–581.

[19] Ibid., 557: "The simplicity of the exegesis which emerges from placing the text in the order that is here adopted is a strong argument in its favour."

[20] Rudolf Bultmann, *The Gospel of John: A Commentary* (Philadelphia: Westminster, 1971), 461, 485–486.

From his point of view the prayer should stand before the discourse, not after it, since it functions as a companion piece to the parting meal. Bultmann said that it would follow most naturally from the first clause of 13:31, at which point Judas the betrayer is dismissed, and Jesus is left in the intimate company of his closest circle of friends.[21]

> The structure of the whole complex—on the basis of the new order—is very simple. 13:1–30 records Jesus' last meal with his disciples; 17:1–26 gives us the farewell prayer; 13:31–35; 15–16:33; 13:36–14:31 contain the farewell discourses and conversations.[22]

The theses of Bernard and Bultmann are fairly standard expressions of this form of diachronic reading of John 13–17. Both Bernard and Bultmann find the "rough"-ness alluded to by Ashton occurring in that they sense that the text in its present form is a crudely edited stitching together of disconnected pieces. For each, the questions of literary anomalies (repetitions, abrupt interruptions, logic disjunctures) within the discourse as it has been received are resolved by placing chapters 15–16 before the conversations at the close of chapter 13. In this manner the command to "rise and leave" in 14:31 becomes the final discourse statement made by Jesus, preparing the way for the action at the onset of chapter 18.

The second diachronic view of the materials of the farewell discourse sees in these chapters a record of the changing historical circumstances that engaged the Johannine community. The rough form of the text is the result of accretions to the discourse as a result of multiple redactions. These redactions either gathered materials that had previously existed for unique hortatory reasons in other contexts in order to provide a broader exhortation for the church, or they added newly written materials that responded to the changing threats experienced by the faith community as it moved through different developmental stages.

Pryor takes the former approach. His divisions of the farewell discourse are as follows:[23]

---

[21] Ibid., 486–487.

[22] Ibid., 461.

[23] John W. Pryor, *John: Evangelist of the Covenant People* (Downers Grove, Illinois: InterVarsity Press, 1992), 103.

1. Prelude to the discourses
   - 13:1–20 Footwashing and its lessons
   - 13:21–38 Further dialogue on the betrayal and departure
2. Discourse 1
   - 14:1–31 Jesus' departure and return
3. Discourse 2
   - 15:1–17 The vine and branches: obedience to Christ and commitment to one another
   - 15:18–16:4a Obedience to Christ brings persecution
4. Discourse 3
   - 16:4b–33 The ongoing presence among his own of Christ the departed one
5. Final Prayer
   - 17:1–26

Pryor surveys the interpretive options available, noting the reasons to consider this discourse as a composite whole,[24] but rejecting solutions that either rearrange the given materials or psychologize the obvious disruptions away.[25] He then draws another conclusion:

> ...in chapters 13–17 we are presented with a self-consciously integrated whole discourse, which, like Deuteronomy, is the farewell word of the mediator of the covenant to the people of God. It gives teaching, instruction and encouragement for the covenant people in their life after the departure of Jesus. But the whole is actually a bringing together of units and discourses, from the same author, which were originally separate. Modification has taken place for the purpose of integration into the gospel.[26]

Painter also assumes that all of the discourse material was written by the same author, but in various smaller units. He believes these were collected into their present form over a period of decades, as the Johannine community grew through several evolutionary stages in its unfolding life.[27] The experiences of the first major period of the

---

[24] Ibid., 102–3.

[25] Ibid., 104–6.

[26] Ibid., 106.

[27] Painter, *Quest*, 417–435.

community, reflecting on its desire for an intimate relationship with Jesus, produced chapters 13–14, followed immediately by what are designated as chapters 18–20 in the present form of the text. The purpose for the discourse in that stage, as the emphasis on the παράκλητος in chapter 14 suggests, was to encourage the faith community to cope with the delay in Jesus' returning by focusing on the comfort and instruction brought through the Spirit. At this stage in the community's history, the material of chapters 15–17 was not yet written, though it may possibly have existed in seminal form in oral tradition.

As the Johannine community experienced persecution (and possible expulsion from the Jewish synagogue) around 80 CE, a second version of the farewell discourse was added, positioned after 14:31. This rendition (15:1–16:4a) included a speech by Jesus that specifically prophesied a coming persecution, and further expressed the comfort brought by the παράκλητος ("Advocate") in even stronger terms. A third version of the discourse was added later (16:4b–16:33), responding to the abandonment the community experienced as the tide of persecution passed and Jesus still failed to return. The prayer of John 17 was later added to the discourse, after the three versions had already been collected in their final form.

Though Painter's hypotheses are attractive in their attempt to document the life cycles of the Johannine community and in their desire to root the gospel in expressions of historical need, there are some clear limitations to the view. First of all, Painter's approach does not explain how the report of a single event could be given in such different forms by the same author.[28] Secondly, Painter does not indicate why the present literary sequence of teachings is better than another arrangement of the same materials.[29] Still, Painter's view does provide a cogent reason for the troublesome literary disjunctures, while at the same time offering a realistic interpretation for the flow and meaning of the discourse as it now stands.

Synchronic Perspectives

In contrast to these "rough" readings of John 13–17, which focus on the disjunctures in the text and the supposed historical

---

[28] Ibid.
[29] Ibid., 417–418.

developments that produced the various sections of the discourse, there is another family of approaches that begins with the assumption that the text as it stands has literary integrity. When, in interpretive approaches that Ashton identifies as "narrative criticism,"[30] the Johannine farewell discourse is given a "smooth" or synchronic reading, two other interpretive paradigms emerge.

The first simply declares that there is no problem with the text in its present shape. Jesus would naturally repeat himself. This is typical of any normal conversation revolving around a thematic discussion. Further, the call to exit in 14:31 only means that chapters 15 and 16 were spoken as the group rose and cloaked in preparation for leaving,[31] or as they strolled together through the Kidron valley,[32] or perhaps past the Temple,[33] with Jesus using the vineyards or the gilded vines ornamenting the Temple as object lessons.

The second synchronic approach to the farewell discourse worries less about the temporal framework surrounding the text, and focuses more on the intellectual and spiritual issues at stake. It supposes that all elements of the discourse which might, at a casual glance, seem unusual or disruptive to the typical flow of a continuous conversation such as this is portrayed to be, are actually cues expressing movement from one plane of thought to another. When Jesus urges his disciples to rise and leave, he is guiding them to a higher plateau of existence.

Brodie explains this view well.[34] Although the command to rise and leave at the end of 14:31 could be viewed merely as the abrupt conclusion of an earlier textual source, no editor who takes the time to put together such a focused collection of teachings would permit it to stay at that point in the finished product. It would be far easier, says Brodie, to move that phrase to either the end of chapter 16 or the end of chapter 17, as long as pieces were being stitched together anyway.

---

[30] Ashton, *Studying John*, 140–165.

[31] William Hendriksen, *The New Testament Commentary: Exposition of the Gospel According to John* (Grand Rapids: Baker, 1953), 290; Leon Morris, *The Gospel According to John* (Grand Rapids: Eerdmans, 1971), 661.

[32] D. A. Carson, *The Gospel According to John* (Grand Rapids: Eerdmans, 1991), 479.

[33] B. F. Westcott, *The Gospel According to St. John* (Grand Rapids: Eerdmans, 1954), 187; Ernst Haenchen, *A Commentary on the Gospel of John* (Philadelphia: Fortress, 1984), 128.

[34] Brodie, *Gospel*, 437–440.

Rather than viewing the command at the close of chapter 14 as an unfortunate editorial oversight, Brodie claims to put forward a far better interpretation. The author of the Fourth Gospel, according to Brodie, meant for this stirring command to occur exactly where it is. Its point, he says, is to signal a movement within the developments of the conversations, elevating the next section (beginning at 15:1) to a higher dimension of spiritual awareness. In fact, says Brodie, there are exactly two such brief suggestions of movement throughout the entire discourse following the meal. This command to rise and leave at the end of chapter 14 is the first. A second occurs at the outset of chapter 17 when the attention of the reader is turned, by the change of focus in Jesus' own words, upward toward heaven.

For Brodie, each of these is significant in that each announces the next stage in the spiritual journey charted by the farewell discourse. The command in 14:31 "lays the emphasis on a form of departure, on a leaving of the past ('...from here'),"[35] while "the second places the focus on a form of arrival, on coming fully to God ('...to heaven')."[36] In other words, Jesus begins the discourse where the disciples already find themselves, attached as they are to the mundane affairs of their daily existence. Jesus challenges them to leave these things of lesser importance behind, just as he is about to (chapters 13–14). Through his exhortation Jesus is able to focus the hearts of the disciples sufficiently so that they are able to set the earthly matters of their past behind and rise, with Jesus, to the second level of spiritual maturity. This is signalled in the vine and branches teaching. If they remain connected to him, no matter what their circumstances, these followers of Jesus will experience his strengthening and comfort (chapters 15–16). Finally, once assured of these things, Jesus' disciples are ready to move on to the ultimate spiritual plane. With Jesus, in 17:1, they turn their eyes toward heaven and the future, and he strengthens their metaphysical union with himself and the Father by way of the prayer of chapter 17.

Brodie says that the Fourth Gospel often uses physical movement indicators to mark divisions of the text into sections of meaning.[37] Further, he declares that the elements of repetition in the

---

[35] Ibid., 437.

[36] Ibid.

[37] He cites the movement around the pool in John 9, and the command of Jesus to the Samaritan woman in chapter 4 ("Go call your husband and come here") as similar occurrences.

discourse are typical of poetic emphasis and variation, and not the result of poor editing. Also, the statement of Jesus in chapter 16 that no one is asking him where he is going, even though Peter and Thomas had already done so, is another cue that further affirms his thesis of successive planes of spiritual elevation. Since the disciples should have experienced growth and maturation as they followed Jesus on the pilgrimage moving from chapters 13–14 to 15–16, it saddens Jesus when he sees that they do not seem to make as much progress as he had hoped. Jesus' lament at 16:5–6 indicates the changing somber mood of the discussion. Jesus is becoming disheartened, and is unsure that his followers will be able to make the leap to a higher plane. His cry is intended to rouse them to the task in a shocking challenge.

What Brodie has done is to insist that the received form of the text must stand with integrity and meaning. It may have been produced through a process of compilation, but any discussions regarding its redactive history or the changing circumstances of the community from which it emerged are not important for present interpretation. Instead, whatever appear to be problematic issues in the text as it stands need to be resolved in ways that require no explanation beyond the text itself. Indeed, segmenting the text in search of previous versions only detracts from a fuller investigation of the literary clues that were imbedded in the existing discourse.

Evaluation

While each of these approaches has some merit, none is entirely satisfactory. On the one hand, the diachronic reading of the Fourth Gospel results in a plethora of interpretive possibilities that seem to have little relationship with one another, and sometimes undermine or overlook any meaning the text might have as it stands. The dislocation theory of Bernard and Bultmann, for example, results in an extremely subjective interpretation of the farewell discourse, since there can be no final arbiter of correct repositioning of its elements.[38] Painter's analysis of stages of development may explain disruptions in the text, but it argues tautologically in arriving at focus and meaning. If the second discourse emerged from a sharp conflict in the synagogue, then this would be the resulting exhortation. The former may be read from the latter, however, as easily as the latter may be read from the former.

---

[38] Cf. Carson, *Gospel*, 480.

Further, why should a single author pen significantly different accounts of the same incident, and then splice them together so poorly? Beside, what reason would there be for having the three discourses appear in chronological order, when, over the course of time, a thematic arrangement would probably provide a better exhortation for the community?[39]

When evaluating the synchronic approaches, other questions surface. The "discourse on the way" may explain the unusual positioning of Jesus' command at the end of 14:31, but it does not adequately address the repetition of very similar ideas and phrases that are gathered on either side of 15:1–17. Why should the discussion turn back in on itself in chapter 16, when the movement of the group has already pushed the thematic issues ahead? Nor is it likely that the prayer of chapter 17 would be uttered while the group is in motion in public places. Even with the shelter of night or the devotional surroundings of the Temple precincts, the prayer is too intimate and follows too closely from the meal table discussion to be separated from the context expressed in the early verses of chapter 13.

Further, the psychological elevation theory fails to read 14:31 in its most natural way. True, other discourses of Jesus in the Fourth Gospel are often convoluted and repetitious,[40] and are usually bracketed by brief notes of spatial or temporal movement. However, a psychological reading of the movement in 14:31 would require an unusual interpretation of the words (understanding them as inviting spiritual elevation rather than physical movement) in a context that does not clearly call for such a drastic shift. Also, there is little evidence that the discourse materials of chapters 15–16 are necessarily of a higher philosophic or spiritual character than those of chapters 13–14.[41] Likewise, the prayer of chapter 17 seems an unusual way to take the three-stage discipleship discourse to its final phase.

As Ashton advised, both synchronic and diachronic approaches to the Fourth Gospel have insights to offer.[42] He hoped that someday

---

[39] Cf. Pryor, *John*, 106.

[40] E.g., the "bread of life" discourse in 6:25–59, the "Father" testimony and his relation to his "children" in 8:12–59.

[41] Particularly when Brodie interprets Jesus' statement that no one asks where he is going in 16:5–6 as a dark moment of disbelief (Brodie, *Gospel*, 440).

[42] Ashton, *Studying John*, 141–165, 185–208.

there would be an approach that would take both into account.[43] He believed that this new approach would provide a broader understanding of the Fourth Gospel as it now exists than seems possible when scholarship is limited to a polarisation of choice only between the two.[44] It is in the context of this polarisation that Segovia argues for a new reading of the farewell discourse, one that sees the two readings as complementing each other.[45] In his search for such an approach, he points with some enthusiasm to the insights of Yves Simoens,[46] and his chiastic interpretation of John 13–17.[47]

Interpretive Issues

Segovia's challenge and Simoens' approach (which will be reviewed later in this thesis) bring us back to the central issues addressed by this dissertation. A chiastic reading of John 13–17, as outlined earlier in this chapter and defended in the pages that follow, can bring together the insights of both synchronic and diachronic approaches to the Johannine farewell discourse.

There are a number of issues that must be addressed in order to defend this thesis. For one thing, chiasm, as a literary device, must be explained and understood in biblical and extra–biblical literature. Second, although there is broad agreement on the function and expression of micro-chiasm in biblical literature, the case must be made that macro-chiasm is also expressed in passages of greater length like that of the Johannine farewell discourse, since not all scholars agree that chiasm can function on any but the micro-chiasm level. Third, the criteria for finding and evaluating macro-chiasm need

---

[43] For that reason Ashton included, in the second edition of his editorial collection, *The Interpretation of John* (Edinburgh: T & T Clark, 1997), M. C. DeBoer's article on "Narrative Criticism, Historical Criticism, and the Gospel of John," 301–314, first published in *Journal for the Study of the New Testament* 45 (1992): 35–48.

[44] Cf. also Philip B. Horner, *Relation Analysis of the Fourth Gospel: A Study in Reader-Response Criticism* (Lewiston, New York: Mellen Biblical Press, 1993), 158–161.

[45] Segovia, *Farewell*, 283–329.

[46] Ibid., 37–40.

[47] Yves Simoens, *La Gloire d'aimer: Structures stylistiques et interprétatives dans la Discours de la Cène (Jn 13–17)*, AnBib 90 (Rome: Biblical Institute, 1981).

careful delineation in order that a passage like the Johannine farewell discourse can be assessed chiastically according to meaningful standards. Fourth, there must be a careful exegetical analysis of John 13–17 to determine appropriate literary sections, development, and interrelated character. Fifth, evaluation of other viable chiastic interpretations must be offered in order to demonstrate the strength of the chiastic structure proposed here. Finally, these investigations should offer insights into old exegetical puzzles and bring divergent interpretative approaches together in a new synthesis.

Structure of the Thesis

In order to accomplish these tasks I begin with an investigation of the current state of chiastic studies (Part I). This will incorporate a review of the expression of chiasm as a rhetorical device in the literatures of antiquity generally (Chapter 2), as well as a distillation of the criteria that have been put forward for assessing chiastic readings, including a delineation of the criteria used in this study (Chapter 3).

In Part II, I will offer a brief survey of micro-chiasm in both the Hebrew Bible and the New Testament (Chapter 4). Then I will explore at greater length the question of the legitimacy of macro-chiasm and show the manner in which the criteria proposed in Chapter 3 relate to assessments of chiasm on the macro-chiasm scale (Chapter 5).

Finally, in Part III, I will begin the search for macro-chiasm in the Johannine farewell discourse by rehearsing the plot of John 13–17, looking for repetitions, reflexive parallelism, and centring (Chapter 6). These movements will then be tested against the criteria for assessing macro-chiasm that were identified in Chapter 3 (Chapter 7). Several other attempts at a chiastic reading of the Johannine farewell discourse will be discussed (Chapter 8) before a concluding summary in which this analysis is shown to provide new insights into a number of interpretive difficulties (Chapter 9).

While the reading of the Johannine farewell discourse presented here supersedes the one begun in 1986, it is very much rooted in that naïve beginning. Not only does it provide a reading of the discourse that addresses the usual interpretive difficulties in John 13–17 in a fresh way, but it also suggests a way to bring together traditional diachronic and synchronic approaches in a synthesis that does justice to the concerns of each perspective.

PART I

THE CURRENT STATE OF CHIASTIC STUDIES

CHAPTER 2

CHIASM IN THE LITERATURE OF ANTIQUITY

A Quiet Presence

There is no textbook on the background or use of chiasm in antiquity. There are, however, some indications in various sources that seem to point to early developments in the use of chiastic reflexivity. Lausberg's research indicates that the first use of the term "chiasm" occurred at least as far back as the fourth century BCE. Isocrates, an Athenian teacher of oratory who believed that rhetorical prose and speech making ought to be works of art, made reference to chiasm as a reflexive tool that repeated an idea in inverse order, using different words for effect.[1] In his collections of model speeches,[2] designed to provide patterns of recitation and discourse for his students, as well as for some of the leading political figures of his day,[3] Isocrates attempted to elevate oral communication into artistic expression.[4] His use of chiasm in political speechmaking and in training students of oratory seems to indicate that chiastic reflexivity may have originated in oral communication, finding its way from public address to the written page when stylized speeches were written down for theatrical or historical uses.

---

[1] H. Lausberg, *Handbuch der literarischen Rhetorik* (Munich: Universität Drukerpresse, 1960), 893.

[2] *Panegyricus* (c. 380 BCE); *Plataicus* (c. 373 BCE); *Archidamus* (c. 366 BCE); *Symachicus* (c. 341 BCE); *Areopagticus* (c. 354 BCE); *Panathenaicus* (c. 339 BCE).

[3] Archidamus, king of Sparta, and Philip II of Macedonia, in particular.

[4] Cf. Michael Grant, *The Classical Greeks* (New York: Scribners, 1989), 220–223.

Such practices of Greek rhetoric appear to be confirmed in statements made by Cicero in the first century BCE. In his drama *Atticus*, the main character asks two questions about the verdict of the trial of Clodius (1, 16, 1). Cicero develops the dialogue so that the second question is answered first, then the first question. More than that, Cicero testifies that he deliberately fashions the response in this manner because of the example set by Homer.[5]

It was some time, however, before there was a clear reference to the designation of chiasm as a technical classification for a rhetorical method. According to Kennedy, the first certain use of this expression appears to be that of Hermogenes in his essay "On Invention" (4.3), in the late fourth century of the Common Era.[6] There Hermogenes identifies chiasm as the crosswise interchange of the clauses in a four-clause sentence.

A Miscellany of Evidence

While this limited number of references to the term "chiasm" in classical literature does not provide a broad framework for building a theory of chiastic expression as an ancient rhetorical tool, there is other evidence that must be considered. For one thing, as Thomson pointed out, ancient theories of rhetoric often vacillated between using Greek and Latin nomenclature.[7] He showed how a variety of terms and definitions in Latin signified essentially the same rhetorical movements as that of the Greek idea of chiasm. His research pointed to expressions like *"commutatio"* (the passing along of a thought to another expression at a later location in the passage), *"figurae"* (typification of an idea to serve as reference in another expression), *"inclusio"* (returning to an earlier thought at the close of a particular pericope), *"regressio"* (the "retreating" of a line of thought along the same path taken in previous sentences). These, he said, were shown by Roman commentators Servius and Donatus to have an equivalent value to the

---

[5] Cf. Augustine Stock, "Chiastic Awareness and Education in Antiquity," *Biblical Theology Bulletin* 14 (1984): 23–27.

[6] G. A. Kennedy, *New Testament Interpretation through Rhetorical Criticism* (Chapel Hill, North Carolina: University of North Carolina Press, 1984), 28.

[7] Thomson, *Chiasmus*, 14.

Greek expression ὕστερον πρότερον (an argument that reverses natural or rational order, making first last, and last first).[8] Each of these, according to Thomson, is essentially the same as an aspect of what we today call chiasm. Indeed, Aristarchus of Alexandria (c. 215–143 BCE) actually used the phrase ὕστερον πρότερον[9] in a specific comparison with *"chiasmus,"* defining the former as an inversion of ideas and the latter as the inversion of actual words.[10] He himself noted at least one obvious incidence of chiasm in Homer's Odyssey.[11] As Odysseus makes his way through the underworld in a quest for information about the route he and his men should take in order to return home, he encounters the shade of Anticleia, his mother. Homer pens a conversation in which Odysseus asks his mother's shade a series of questions:[12]

> How she had died,
>> Was it by a long disease,
>> Or by the gentle arrows of Artemis?
> He asks about his father,
>> And about his son;
>> He asks whether a stranger had assumed royal power,
>> And about his own wife, where does she stay?

In a clear expression of chiasm, Homer has the shade of Anticleia respond to this interrogation with a counter series of statements that occur in an exact reversal of the order in which Odysseus asked his questions. Says the shade of Anticleia:[13]

> She stays in your halls;
> No man has taken your royal honours;
> Telemachus farms the estate,
> And your father remains in the countryside, longing for
>> your return.

---

[8] Cf. also Stock, "Chiastic Awareness," 27.
[9] Ibid.
[10] See J. W. Welch, editor, *Chiasmus in Antiquity: Structures, Analyses, Exegesis* (Hildesheim: Gerstenberg, 1981), 255.
[11] Oxyrhyncus Papyrus 1086.
[12] *The Odyssey*, 11.169–183.
[13] *The Odyssey*, 11.184–201.

  Artemis did not slay me with her gentle arrows,
  Nor did a sickness,
  But I died of longing for you.

The parallel of terms and reversal of order are impeccably clear. It appears, in this passage, that Homer uses the reflexive repetition of terms and ideas in chiastic development to highlight the significance of Odysseus' wife remaining faithful, while providing a complete response to all of Odysseus' concerns about his village and kin.

This incidence of chiasm is not an orphan without siblings in the world of ancient literature. In his survey of classical literature, Kennedy comes to the conclusion that chiasm in both simple and elaborate forms is prevalent throughout Greek literature from as early as these representations in the writings of Homer.[14]

Yet it remains somewhat disconcerting that, even with these and other expressions of chiasm, little is said about chiasm as a rhetorical device by either classical rhetoricians or more recent literary critics. Noting this unusual neglect, Thomson speculates that such a void might be caused by a pervasive assumption that chiasm is a "compositional technique" rather than a polished rhetorical device.[15] He contends that chiasm was practised in common expressions of story-telling, and that students of classical rhetoric were often encouraged to distance themselves from these vulgar conventions in order to display their more learned skills. For this reason the discipline of rhetoric would avoid references to commonplace chiasm as it pursued more advanced or enlightened forms of communication.

If Thomson is correct in his claim, the absence of references to chiasm in a general way throughout classic rhetoric is a result of intentional neglect rather than non-existence of the technique itself. Since chiasm was part of the practice of storytelling in marketplace and home, academic training in speech disciplines needed nomenclature for similar forms of reflexive speech development that superseded the ordinary, and gave them more suitable cultured recognition.

Of course, an argument from silence is difficult either to prove or disprove. Still, the examples noted of ancient narrative passages that appear to be chiastically developed provide at least preliminary evidence that micro-chiasm was a literary tool in use among writers in several cultures of the Mediterranean world. Further, as Kennedy

---

[14] Kennedy, *New Testament Interpretation*, 28–29.
[15] Thomson, *Chiasmus,* 17.

notes, classical rhetoricians used the Latin term *commutatio* to describe simple reflexive patterns among lines of poetry and prose of the a–b–b–a form.[16] Certainly, as we shall see in Chapter 4, the incidence of micro-chiasm throughout the literature of the Hebrew Bible is both widespread and obvious.

---

[16] Kennedy, *New Testament Interpretation*, 28.

CHAPTER 3

THE ESSENTIALS OF CHIASM

Non-Linear Communication

It is important, at this point, to determine more specifically the criteria by which chiasm in biblical literature will be assessed. Although there are clear representations of chiasm scattered throughout the literature of antiquity, it was not until early in the twentieth century, largely through the work of Lund, that chiastic analyses in biblical studies were more widely developed.

While he was a student at North Park Theological Seminary in Chicago, Lund began an investigation that would ultimately become a lifetime passion, namely, to observe and specify the use of chiasm as a New Testament literary convention. From 1929 through 1934 Lund published a series of seven articles on various aspects of the topic.[1] At the same time he was working on a much more comprehensive investigation of chiasm in its historical and biblical expressions. This monograph would eventually become his Ph.D. dissertation for the University of Chicago.[2] In it Lund devoted himself to "the tracing of

---

[1] Nils W. Lund, "The Presence of Chiasmus in the Old Testament," *American Journal of Semitic Languages and Literature* 46 (1929–1930), 104–126; "The Presence of Chiasmus in the New Testament," *Journal of Religion* 10 (1930), 74–93; "The Influence of Chiasmus upon the Structure of the Gospels," *Anglican Theological Review* 13 (1931), 27–48; "The Influence of Chiasmus upon the Structure of the Gospel according to Matthew," *Anglican Theological Review* 13 (1931), 405–433; "The Literary Structure of Paul's Hymn to Love," *Journal of Biblical Literature* 50 (1931), 266–276; "Chiasmus in the Psalms," *American Journal of Semitic Languages and Literature* 49 (1932–1933), 281–312; "The Literary Structure of the Book of Habakkuk," *Journal of Biblical Literature* 53 (1934), 355–370.

[2] Nils W. Lund, *Chiasmus in the New Testament: A Study in the Formgeschichte* (Chapel Hill: University of North Carolina Press, 1942).

the Hebrew literary influence on the Greek text of the New Testament,"[3] with a particular focus on "the extensive use of the inverted order commonly called chiasmus."[4]

In an early article,[5] Lund had outlined what he perceived to be the chiastic structure to the Prologue of the Fourth Gospel. His analysis of that passage continues to be influential for many scholars through to the present.[6] It included the elucidation of elements of chiastic arrangement that Lund would later distil into seven theses:[7]

1. The center of a chiastically shaped pericope is always the turning point.
2. The thought shifts at the center, often to an antithetic thought, only to return to the previous line of argument or topic development.
3. Identical ideas are distributed across the given passage at the extremes and center.
4. Some ideas are redistributed in the second half as if deliberately reiterated.
5. Certain terms appear to gravitate toward the center of the passage.
6. Larger units are frequently introduced and concluded by "frame-passages."
7. Chiastic developments are frequently interspersed with linear progressive lines.

These "laws"[8] are essentially observational hypotheses. Yet they resonate with recurring phenomena in the textual data.[9] For Lund they indicated thought processes at work in both the Hebrew Bible and in the New Testament that consciously highlighted an idea of significance by placing it at the center of a discourse. The normative character of

---

[3] Ibid., 28.

[4] Ibid.

[5] Nils W. Lund, "The Influence of Chiasmus upon the Structure of the Gospels," 27–48.

[6] Cf. R. Alan Culpepper, "The Pivot of John's Prologue," *New Testament Studies* 27 (1981): 1–31; Jeffrey Lloyd Staley, "The Structure of John's Prologue," *Catholic Biblical Quarterly* 48 (1986): 241–264.

[7] Lund, *Chiasmus*, 40–41.

[8] In a review of Lund's book in *Journal of Theological Studies* (45 [1944]: 82), T. W. Manson suggested that the term "law" is excessive.

[9] Thomson, *Chiasmus*, 213–219.

this centered idea in the pericope as a whole was reinforced textually through balanced pairs of inverted parallel complementary statements or themes on either side of it that "pointed" back to it as the structuring motif of the larger passage.

Focus on Repetition and Centering

While Lund's concise "laws" governing chiastic movement within a passage are useful in discerning the broad outlines of chiastic passages,[10] they lack the precision required for careful examination of those texts where chiasm might be suspected as playing a role in the development of themes and concepts in a particular passage.[11]

First of all, as Culpepper noted,[12] Lund's "laws" fail to provide a clear set of criteria for identifying clues that might signal chiastic intent. They document what Lund declares to be the moves of chiasm, but they do not indicate where one begins to look for those moves. Clark worked to fill this void in his 1975 essay, "Criteria for Identifying Chiasm."[13] According to Clark, chiastic repetition, parallelism, and centering may be found in any, several or all of these dimensions of a passage: content, structure, choice of words, setting, and theology.[14] Thus, for Clark, chiasm might be found on several levels of literary expression. Although he does not make entirely clear the precise tools which might be used in assessing each of these dimensions of communication, Clark's analysis of Lund's general search for parallel repetition into several categories broadens the possibilities in the search for chiasm, while, at the same time, it calls for more clarity in describing what sort of parallel is to be found. In addition, Clark observed that most assessments of chiasm are to be evaluated on some cumulative collection of evidence that may be less than fully apparent at the first reading.[15] He offers several different types of measures by which to assess possible chiastic design in a text,

---

[10] Cf. Culpepper, "Pivot," 6–7.

[11] Cf. Porter and Reed, "Philippians as a Macro-Chiasm," 218–219.

[12] Culpepper, "Pivot," 6–7.

[13] David J. Clark, "Criteria for Identifying Chiasm," *Linguistica Biblica* 5 (1975): 63–72.

[14] Ibid., 63.

[15] Ibid., 66. See also Mark Allan Powell, *What Is Narrative Criticism?* (Minneapolis: Fortress, 1990), 32–34; Grant R. Osborne, *The Hermeneutical Spiral* (Downers Grove, Illinois: InterVarsity Press, 1991), 35–40.

especially focusing on locating and isolating repetitions of content within a pericope either in language or structure.[16]

Second, Lund's "laws" fail to explore adequately both the idea of the heightened literary impact of the central element in a chiasm and the importance of balanced length on both sides of this center. Thomson, in rewriting Lund's "laws" and amplifying them to address that need more specifically, suggested the following, more precise, criteria:[17]

1. Chiasms frequently exhibit a shift at, or near, their center. This change can be very varied in nature: a change of person of the verb, a new or unexpected idea suddenly introduced, and so on. Usually, after the 'shift,' the original thought is resumed. For this reason, in this study, the phrase 'shift and reversion' is preferred to Lund's simple term. This immediately highlights the problem associated with all such characteristics. Many passages have 'shifts,' but are obviously not chiastic; in a chiasmus 'shifts' that are not at its center will occur, marking, for example, points of development in an argument.

2. Chiasms are sometimes introduced or concluded by a frame passage. Lund himself makes no comment on this, but, judged by examples which he later gives, a 'frame-passage' is a spring-board from which to launch into the chiasmus, or a section which acts as a tail-piece to a chiasmus without itself being part of the chiastic pattern.

3. Passages which are chiastically patterned sometimes also contain directly parallel elements.[18]

4. Identical ideas may occasionally be distributed in such a fashion that they occur at the extremes of the passage and also again at the center of a given chiastic system.

---

[16] Clark, "Criteria," 68–69.

[17] Thomson, *Chiasmus*, 27.

[18] Lund, according to Thomson, lacks precision in his quest for chiasm by ignoring the obvious possibility of direct parallels between chiastic halves. It is at this point in his rewriting of Lund's criteria that Thomson is beginning to push in the direction of clearly articulated word and phrase parallels as necessary for chiastic design. In this he rejects Lund's thematic parallelism, and with it much of Clark's recommendation regarding the possibility of multi-dimensional layers of chiastic meaning.

5. Balancing elements are normally of approximately the same length. On a few occasions when this is not the case, some explanation seems to be called for.
6. The center often contains the focus of the author's thought. It will be suggested that this is a particularly powerful feature with obvious implications for exegesis.

In light of what Thomson believes are a plethora of unwarranted supposed discoveries of chiasm throughout the New Testament, he elaborates on the use of his guidelines, making a plea for rigorous objectivity by those who seek to assess any passage for possible chiastic development.[19] First, Thomson says, "the chiasmus will be present in the text as it stands, and will not require unsupported textual emendation in order to 'recover' it."[20] Either it is there or it is not, and any attempt to find it in previous redactions of the text only remind us that the form of the passage in its final editing undid whatever chiasm might have been there earlier.

Second, according to Thomson, "the symmetrical elements will be present in precisely inverted order."[21] That is to say, where one must seek to rearrange elements in order to gain parallel inversion of elements in a passage, it is not likely that chiastic intent was there in the first place. Thomson does allow for some latitude in this requirement, so long as the rationale for a departure from the norm makes sense within the development of the passage itself.

Third, says Thomson, "the chiasmus will begin and end at a reasonable point."[22] In other words, the reason for expressing a thought in chiastic design is to define the relationships among the elements of a single subunit of communication, whether it is represented in four short lines of poetry or encompasses a comprehensive tale unfolded in an extended narrative. There must be a correlation between the completeness of the thought unit and the extent or boundaries of the

---

[19] Welch, *Chiasmus in Antiquity*, 13.
[20] Thomson, *Chiasmus*, 28.
[21] Ibid., 29.
[22] Ibid.

chiastically shaped passage. If either moves on before the other, chiasm is not likely to be present at all.[23]

Although it is clear that chiasm is one among many literary forms used in both the Hebrew Bible and the New Testament, it is not always as certain when chiastic patterns are definitively present. According to the criteria established by Clark, chiastic intent in a passage is recognized on the basis of the strength and combination of up to five intermingling elements:

> (1) content—the theme or themes of each pericope, (2) form or structure—the type of narrative and/or dialogue of which the pericope is composed, (3) language—primarily the occurrence [*sic*] of catchwords. ...Two other features... are worth separate listing: (4) setting, and (5) theology.[24]

While these five criteria are the basis for chiastic exploration, they are not sufficiently precise to provide the specific tools of analysis in all instances. As Thomson says, the process for identifying chiasm "is inevitably complex."[25] Not only that, but it appears, at times, to become an exercise in circular reasoning: one reads a passage looking for a particular pattern of repetition or reflexivity; then, when hints of such a pattern are found, one declares that the form of the pattern found is both typical and original. It is typical because it follows the pre-asserted pattern, and it is original in the sense that its form provides the basis upon which to seek further similar patterns.

Pay Attention to Balance and Parallelism

Thomson suggests both a two-step method by which to assess the evidence for chiasm in a text, and a series of carefully delineated guidelines that are designed to shape the process of testing the

---

[23] These criteria, according to Thomson (*Chiasmus*), rule out the more speculative ends to which chiasm has sometimes been pushed, such as "chiasm by headings" without reference to the substance of the text itself (p. 30), the selective use of certain recurring words or thoughts, while bypassing other instances of the same words or thought which simply do not fit the projected chiasm (p. 31), the ignoring of non-balancing elements in a particular passage (pp. 31–32), and using chiasm as a quick answer in situations where other scholarship has failed to reach some degree of consensus in interpretation (p. 32).

[24] Clark, "Criteria," 63.

[25] Thomson, *Chiasmus*, 33.

hypothesis from beginning to end. The first stage in Thomson's investigation is "to identify a pattern which is potentially chiastic."[26] This means that the reader pays attention to repetition of vocabulary and syntax, and seeks the possible inverse paralleling of common words and ideas. Thus, the first step is that of data-collection. Are there triggers in the text that give the reader a reason to pause for a second appraisal, seeking larger patterns of recurring movement? Is there a sudden shift of an idea back along the path recently taken? Do the extremes of a passage reiterate a single idea in some reflexive form?

Secondly, according to Thomson, the suspected chiasm must be put to a critical test involving the use of his criteria for chiasm assessment in a particular manner. The procedure requires movement through the following specific steps:[27]

1. Note whether there is a critical shift at the center of the suspected chiasm which clearly returns the thought back along the path recently taken.
2. Check for the possibility of a "frame passage" which either introduces or concludes a chiastic passage (or perhaps both), clearly setting the chiasm apart from its larger literary environment.
3. Analyse the passage to determine possible subunits of chiastically-aligned elements which are themselves parallel in structure.
4. Extrapolate thematic relationships, realizing that these most often occur at the extremes of the passage, and possibly also at or near the centering element.
5. Check to see whether there is a clear balance of length between the elements of the chiasm that occupy the first half of the design and those which follow the midpoint.
6. Assess the significance of the central element of the passage for the meaning or impact of the passage as a whole. There is most often a heightening and clarification of the main "point" of the narrative or poetic implication in the central element itself. The center, rather than the beginning or ending, holds the interpretive key.

---

[26] Thomson, *Chiasmus*, 33.
[27] Ibid., 27–28.

In response to the increased interest in chiastic studies in recent years, Thomson expresses wary scepticism toward simplistic exegetical efforts that find a plethora of chiastic development throughout biblical texts. He posits several limitations to these investigations that he believes will help scholars looking for chiasm to maintain a necessary academic rigor as they pursue their goals.

For one thing, he holds to the view that chiasm is strictly a device of words and phrases, and not of themes.[28] In this regard he would not agree with Clark that themes might be chiastically arranged in a literary passage, even where the vocabulary and grammar may not appear so. Thomson calls this "chiasmus by headings,"[29] where the reader, rather than the author, views the larger contours of a literary unit and determines a recurrence of themes and ideas. "This produces a potentially circular argument," according to Thomson; "headings are interpretatively selected to create or bolster a chiasmus; it is then argued from the chiasmus that the selective choice of heading reflects the true interests of the author!"[30] There must be a clear correspondence of terms, mirrored across a central axis, according to Thomson, in order for chiasm to be present in a passage.

This leads to the second of Thomson's limitations on the expression of chiasm. As he puts it, the "chiasmus will begin and end at a reasonable point."[31] In his estimation chiasm is generally limited to short passages where clear reflexivity is immediately accessible. The longer the passage, even where repetitions and regressions and *inclusios* are evident in the broader sweep, the more difficult it is to pin down either chiastic intent or the benefits of a chiastic reading.

Thomson is astute in these points. It is important that the paralleled elements of a passage emerge from the passage itself, and are not imposed upon it by way of hopeful thematic projection on the part of the modern interpreter. Also, length certainly plays a crucial role in the clarity of chiastic approbation: the longer a passage is, the harder it becomes to determine whether, or in what clear manner, chiastic design pervades the whole.

What is not immediately apparent, however, is the basis for Thomson's rejection of any chiastic correspondence between themes and ideas that might not exactly repeat certain words or phrases in the

---

[28] Ibid., 30–31.
[29] Ibid., 30.
[30] Ibid., 31.
[31] Ibid., 29.

paired sections of the chiasm. After all, micro-chiastic parallelism in the several lines of a poem often uses different terms to refer to a single thing or idea. It seems probable that, in a similar manner, paired sentences or paragraphs reflecting on common ideas or actions might use different terms or phrases to give shape to these considerations in macro-chiastic developments.

In the same way, there seems to be no clear basis for Thomson's adamant limitation of chiastic length to roughly 15 verses. He offers no reason for denying chiasm to pericopes that extend beyond that arbitrary maximum other than his scepticism at some of the lengthy and seemingly contrived chiastic outlines developed particularly by Lund.

In essence, Thomson rigorously develops criteria for assessing micro-chiasm while denying the possibility of macro-chiasm as a literary device. At issue is whether chiasm is a literary device at work exclusively in relatively brief expressions of reflexive poetic parallelism and quickly told tales, or if it also functions on a broader level as a shaping tool for organizing multiple literary panels. Evidence of the presence of micro-chiasm in biblical poetry and short narrative is well documented.[32] Research into the possibility of identifying macro-chiasm as a literary tool at work in longer, multiple-panel biblical passages abounds,[33] and requires a careful reflection on the relationship between the devices of rhetorical technique and the thought patterns at work in the crafting of narratives.

The heart of the discussion focuses on the question of whether there is a type of pervasive chiastic thought process at work in certain cultures of antiquity that may have resulted, over time, in broadening the range of use of chiastic reflexivity in literary expression. Is it

---

[32] Cf. Umberto Cassuto, "The Chiastic Word Pattern in Hebrew," *Catholic Biblical Quarterly* 38 (1976): 303–311; Umberto Cassuto, "The Function of Chiasmus in Hebrew Poetry," *Catholic Biblical Quarterly* 40 (1978): 1–40; A. di Marco, "Der Chiasmus in der Bibel," *Linguistica Biblica* 36 (1975): 21–79; 37 (1976): 49–68; 44 (1979): 3–70; J. T. Willis, "The Juxtaposition of Synonymous and Chiastic Parallelism in Tricola in Old Testament Hebrew Psalm Poetry," *Vetus Testamentum* 29 (1979): 465–480.

[33] Cf. Peter F. Ellis, *Matthew: His Mind and his Message* (Collegeville: Liturgical Press, 1974); Peter F. Ellis, *Seven Pauline Letters* (Collegeville: Liturgical Press, 1982); Peter F. Ellis, *The Genius of John* (Collegeville: Liturgical Press, 1984); M. Philip Scott, "Chiastic Structure: A Key to the Interpretation of Mark's Gospel," *Biblical Theology Bulletin* 15 (1985): 17–26; Charles Talbert, "Artistry and Theology: An Analysis of the Architecture of Jn 1,19–5,47," *Catholic Biblical Quarterly* 32 (1970): 341–366; Welch, *Chiasmus in Antiquity*.

possible for writers within those cultures to *think* chiastically when developing ideas or narratives, thus producing macro-chiastic patterns of literary development in passages that extend beyond several lines of poetry or single-panel stories?

Regardless of the limits Thomson places on the length of chiastic passages, he believes that chiastic patterns of thinking grew out of the practices of oral recitation and memorization in both the formal and informal training processes of ancient near-eastern cultures. He notes that "even Greek itself at one time was sometimes found written from left to right in one line and from right to left in the next."[34] It is his contention that chiasm is a communicative technique of the "cultural environment"[35] that gave rise to the scriptures of the Hebrew and Christian traditions. He even conjectures that this "ambilateralism" was responsible for a broadened use of chiasm beyond the shorter reflexive parallelism of poetry.[36]

Thomson's work with micro-chiastic studies invites a similar attention to precision and consistency to be paid in macro-chiastic investigations. It suggests, further, that if there are literary movements in a text longer than 15 verses which appear to function in a manner similar to the reflexive parallelism of words in micro-chiasm, these literary movements need to be governed and assessed by criteria that explain both thematic and conceptual parallels as well as grammatical and verbal parallels between the halves of the chiasm.

Extending the Reach: Blomberg on Macro-Chiasm

Porter and Reed would like, with Thomson, to limit the scope of chiastic investigations to short passages that would be termed micro-chiasms. They do not believe that supposed macro-chiasms identified by other scholars are legitimate analyses, since, as they assert, "to date a convincing set of criteria for how to identify chiasm has not been developed."[37] In their view, there are at least three difficulties with the

---

[34] Thomson, *Chiasmus*, 21. As evidence of this βουστροφηδόν he notes extant manuscripts containing copies of Solon's Laws written in this fashion.

[35] Ibid., 22.

[36] Thomson, *Chiasmus*, 22–24. Cf., also, H. I. Marrou, *A History of Education in Antiquity* (New York: Sheed and Ward, 1956); Augustine Stock, "Chiastic Awareness and Education in Antiquity," *Biblical Theology Bulletin* 14 (1984): 23–27.

[37] Porter and Reed, "Philippians as a Macro-Chiasm," 221.

proposals of Lund and Clark.[38] First, "most of the schemes are overly complex, with duplicated or restated criteria." Second, "many of the criteria posited are difficult to quantify." Third, some of the criteria put forward have an "impressionistic" quality about them, resulting in assessments of macro-chiasm that are based largely on what Porter and Reed would term subjective "generalizations."

Porter and Reed rightly argue that unless more objective and measurable criteria are established it will be impossible to use macro-chiasm in a standardized way as an interpretive tool in biblical or classical studies. Their challenge for someone to produce such criteria has already been answered, however, according to Luter and Lee,[39] in theses put forward by Blomberg nearly a decade prior to their request.[40] Concerned that "chiastic outlines have become so fashionable among biblical scholars" without scholarly consensus regarding the "detailed criteria which hypotheses of extended chiasmus must meet in order to be credible," Blomberg proposed "a fairly rigid set of criteria" by which he hoped explorations in macro-chiasm would be assessed.

Blomberg found sufficient documentation of the extensive use of chiasm in the literature of antiquity to move present scholarship beyond a sceptical stance regarding its existence.[41] Further, he believed that chiasm "underlies numerous portions of Scripture where it has not usually been perceived,"[42] since "it was used far more widely in the ancient world than it is today."[43]

---

[38] And with many who attempt chiastic interpretations based upon their methods. Cf., e.g., Ashton, *Studying John*, 153.

[39] A. Boyd Luter and Michelle V. Lee, "Philippians as Chiasmus: Key to the Structure, Unity and Theme Questions," *New Testament Studies* 41 (1995): 89–101.

[40] Craig Blomberg, "The Structure of 2 Corinthians 1–7," *Criswell Theological Review* 4 (1989): 3–20.

[41] Beside Welch, *Chiasmus in Antiquity*, Blomberg points to the "voluminous catalog" of A. di Marco, *Il Chiasmo nella Bibbia* (Torino: Mariettie, 1980).

[42] Blomberg, "Structure," 5.

[43] Ibid. Cf. Thomson (*Chiasmus*, 36): "The fact that modern readers of New Testament Greek may struggle to identify a chiastic structure may say more about the modern cast of mind than about the presence and relevance of chiasmus. It may well be, therefore, that the readers (or even the hearers) of a particular epistle of Paul's would be aware of the presence of chiasmus because of a much more highly developed consciousness of chiastic patterns resulting from its prevalence in the languages of their day." Kenneth E. Bailey (*Poet & Peasant and Through Peasant Eyes* [Grand Rapids: Eerdmans, 1983]) believes that the link between the micro-

He then outlined his criteria for macro-chiasm in nine points, summarized as follows:

1. There must be a problem in perceiving the structure of the text in question, which more conventional outlines fail to resolve... If a more conventional and straightforward structure can adequately account for the textual data, recourse to less obvious arrangements of the material would seem, at the very least, to risk obscuring what was already clear.

2. There must be clear examples of parallelism between the two "halves" of the hypothesized chiasmus, to which commentators call attention even when they propose quite different outlines for the text overall. In other words, the chiasmus must be based on actual verbal repetitions or clear thematic parallels in the text which most readers note irrespective of their overall synthesis. Otherwise it is too simple to see what one wants to see and to impose on the text an alien structural grid.

3. Verbal (or grammatical) parallelism as well as conceptual (or structural) parallelism should characterize most if not all of the corresponding pairs of subdivisions. The repetitive nature of much biblical writing makes it very easy for general themes to recur in a variety of patterns.

4. The verbal parallelism should involve central or dominant imagery or terminology, not peripheral or trivial language. Ancient writers often employed key terms as catchwords to

---

chiasm of literary technique and the macro-chiasm of narrative has its origins in the art of storytelling, and the manner in which oral recitations have a tendency to come full circle in thought processes from beginning to end. First, chiastic inversion (repetition of terms and ideas across a midpoint) and *inclusio* (returning to an original expression or its variation to bring a tale to completion) aids in memorization. With its balance of related words, themes, and sentence structure chiasm offers a way to organize and connect the elements of a prose or poetic recitation. Where details of a story must be carried along from generation to generation in the mind rather than on paper, this becomes very important. Second, chiastically developed thought is primarily inductive rather than deductive. No "thesis" is stated at the beginning, to be aided and supported by syllogistic logic. Instead, the "point" of the narrative approaches in measured anticipation, and then is brought back to its home turf with deepened insight. Third, there is inherent artistic beauty to chiastically ordered communication. The skill of the storyteller is at stake. Both a well-told story and the apparent sagacity of its teller are a product of practice and repetition.

link passages together, although the material they considered central does not always match modern preconceptions of what is important.

5. Both the verbal and conceptual parallelisms should use words and ideas not regularly found elsewhere within the proposed chiasmus. Most unpersuasive proposals fail to meet this criterion; while the pairings suggested may be plausible, a little ingenuity can demonstrate equally close parallelism between numerous other pairs of passages which do not support a chiastic whole.

6. Multiple sets of correspondences between passages opposite each other in the chiasmus as well as multiple members of the chiasmus itself are desirable. A simple ABA' or ABB'A' pattern is so common to so many different forms of rhetoric that it usually yields few startlingly profound insights. Three or four members repeated in inverse sequence may be more significant. Five or more elements paired in sequence usually resist explanations which invoke subconscious or accidental processes.

7. The outline should divide the text at natural breaks which would be agreed upon even by those proposing very different structures to account for the whole. If a proposed chiasmus frequently violates the natural "paragraphing" of the text which would otherwise emerge, then the proposal becomes less probable.

8. The center of the chiasm, which forms its climax, should be a passage worthy of that position in light of its theological or ethical significance. If its theme were in some way repeated in the first and last passages of the text, as is typical in chiasmus, the proposal would become that much more plausible.

9. Finally, ruptures in the outline should be avoided if at all possible. Having to argue that one or more of the members of the reverse part of the structure have been shifted from their corresponding locations in the forward sequence substantially weakens the hypothesis; in postulating chiasmus, exceptions disprove the rule![44]

---

[44] Luter and Lee ("Philippians as Chiasmus") adopt these criteria as the basis for their investigation of a chiastic structure to Philippians, though their examples of "clear parallelism between the two 'halves' of the chiasm" (criterion

Blomberg's criteria for macro-chiasm show great care and insight. They retain the emphasis on strong parallelism and reflexivity present in Thomson's criteria for micro-chiasm, as well as the emphasis on the heightened significance of the central element, and the clear limits of the chiastic passage. At the same time they recognize the possibility of "conceptual (or structural)" parallelism (criterion #4) which is an essential element of macro-chiasms, stretching beyond the simple verbal reflexivity and parallelism of micro-chiasms.

Blomberg, in fact, shows how these criteria function in an assessment of 2 Corinthians 1:12–7:16. He outlines the passage chiastically in the following manner:

A 1:12–22—the Corinthians can rightfully boast in Paul

B 1:23–2:13—grief and comfort over the painful letter; hope for forgiving the offender

C 2:12–13—looking for Titus in Macedonia

D 2:14–4:6—a series of contrasts—belief vs. unbelief, centered on Christians as the letters of the living God, in glory being transformed into his image

E 4:7–5:10—surviving and triumphing despite every hardship

F 5:11–21—the theological climax: the ministry of reconciliation

E' 6:1–10—surviving and triumphing despite every hardship

D' 6:11–7:4—a series of contrasts—belief vs. unbelief, centered on Christians as the temple of the living God, in light being transformed into his holiness

---

#2) are not convincing, at best, their statement of the divisions of the text seems somewhat arbitrary (criterion #7), and the use of the Pauline "travelogue" in Philippians 2:17–3:1 as the "climax" of the chiastic development (criterion #8) presents a strange twist on the usual interpretations of the letter. Indeed, rather than disproving the value of Blomberg's criteria for chiastic assessment they have affirmed it, indicating the manner in which it appears to undermine their own attempt at macro-chiastic analysis.

C' 7:5–7—finding Titus in Macedonia

B' 7:8–13a—grief and comfort over the painful letter; joy after
forgiving the offender

A' 7:13b–16—Paul can rightfully boast in the Corinthians[45]

When reviewing this literary development against his nine criteria for the assessment of macro-chiasm, all points are met. He also reviews briefly a number of other supposed chiastic analyses of other passages which conform to all, some, or a few of these criteria, and thus show varying degrees of success or failure in providing beneficial interpretations.[46]

Porter and Reed agree that Blomberg's criteria "improve upon" Clark's six-point revision of Lund's "laws,"[47] and they find Blomberg's first criterion "particularly relevant,"[48] yet they retain an overall sceptical stance against any assessment of macro-chiasm in biblical literature.[49] Porter and Reed see a "conflict" between the first criterion and the common concerns of criteria 2 and 6. They assume that no scholar could acknowledge parallel developments in a passage and then not provide some satisfactory structure for organizing the materials of the whole.[50] That, of course, has not been the case in a number of New Testament passages, most notably the book of James, where much effort has been given to ascertaining meaningful structure for the commonly perceived repetitive and parallel elements, usually with inconclusive results.[51]

Further, when responding to Blomberg's seventh and ninth criteria (requiring any chiastic interpretation of a text to follow natural literary breaks), Porter and Reed assume that if the breaks in a text are natural this fact necessarily means that chiastic interpretation is not

---

[45] Blomberg, "Structure," 8–9.

[46] Ibid., 7–8.

[47] Porter and Reed, "Philippians as a Macro-Chiasm," 220.

[48] Ibid., 219.

[49] Ibid., 221.

[50] Ibid.

[51] Cf., e.g., Peter H. Davids, *The Epistle of James: a Commentary on the Greek Text* (Grand Rapids: Eerdmans, 1982), 22–29. Interestingly, Davids suggests that a type of chiastic ordering may be helpful in finding a meaningful relationship between the parallel themes and terms occurring in the letter.

necessary.[52] As Blomberg has demonstrated in his review of the issues surrounding the interpretation of 2 Corinthians 1–7, this is simply not the case: "although every division in the proposed chiasmus appears as a major or minor break in the Nestle-Aland Greek NT and is supported by various commentaries,"[53] no other analysis of textual development has proven widely agreeable. It is, in fact, because "Paul's logic contains regular transitional paragraphs which can easily be taken as either concluding a previous thought or beginning a new thought" that no suitable linear understanding of the passage has emerged.[54] Similarly, as we shall see in Chapters 6–9, common recognition of literary shifts in the Johannine farewell discourse has not brought a common sense of structure, and has, indeed, for some, suggested an investigation into chiastic ordering of these passages.

Blomberg's criteria for assessing macro-chiasm appear to provide a reasonable and thorough measure by which to determine the possible existence and scope of chiastic paralleling in biblical and other texts. To date there are no assessment criteria that exceed Blomberg's in either specificity or cohesiveness. Some, like Porter and Reed, or Thomson, might argue with Blomberg that chiasm exists only on the micro level of 12–15 lines at maximum, and limit chiastic reflexive parallelism only to exact verbal or grammatical repetitions. If, however, as many others allow, chiastic reflexivity can also occur on a macro level of paralleled concepts and structures in narrative development, Blomberg's criteria are specific enough to guard against the excesses of those who would impose such outlines on the text rather than reading them from the actual content of each passage.

Chiastic Interpretation

Although chiastic studies reflect primarily on the literature of antiquity, especially focusing on biblical texts, the era of chiastic scholarship has taken shape in a disciplined manner only in the second half of the twentieth century. Lund pioneered a needed investigation of a literary device too long neglected by biblical scholars; Thomson has given necessary precision and clarity to the criteria for assessing

[52] Porter and Read, "Philippians as a Macro-Chiasm," 220.
[53] Blomberg, "Structure," 9–10, 14.
[54] Blomberg, "Structure," 14.

micro-chiasm; and Blomberg, more recently, has advanced suitable criteria for those who believe that chiasm functions on a macro level in certain biblical texts.

In the next section we shall investigate the criteria for assessing chiasm more extensively, exploring passages in both the Hebrew Bible and the New Testament for examples of micro-chiasm (Chapter 4), and then testing Blomberg's criteria, in particular, on passages that appear to exhibit traits of macro-chiasm (Chapter 5).

PART II

FROM MICRO-CHIASM TO MACRO-CHIASM

IN BIBLICAL TEXTS

CHAPTER 4

MICRO-CHIASM IN BIBLICAL INTERPRETATION

The Art of Poetic Reflexivity

The art of micro-chiasm in both the Hebrew Bible and in the New Testament has been extensively documented.[1] In its simplest expressions chiasm appears to be a more complex form of poetic parallelism.[2]

---

[1] For a general treatment see di Marco, "Der Chiasmus in der Bibel," and Welch, *Chiasm in Antiquity*. A less satisfactory compilation, though still containing many helpful examples, is Breck, *Shape*. For a concise overview of chiastic expression in the Hebrew Bible see Nicholas H. Ridderbos and Herbert M. Wolf, "Poetry, Hebrew," *The International Standard Bible Encyclopedia* (Grand Rapids: Eerdmans, 1986): 891–898 (especially 895) and William Sanford La Sor, David Allan Hubbard, and Frederic William Bush, *Old Testament Survey* (Grand Rapids: Eerdmans, 1982), 307–315 (especially 312). More extended discussions occur in Umberto Cassuto, "The Chiastic Word Pattern in Hebrew," 303–311; Umberto Cassuto, "The Function of Chiasmus in Hebrew Poetry," 1–40. A more extensive treatment of chiasm in the Psalms may be found in R. L. Alden, "Chiastic Psalms: A Study in the Mechanics of Semitic Poetry in Psalms 1–50," *Journal of the Evangelical Theological Society* 17 (1974): 11–28 and J. T. Willis, "The Juxtaposition of Synonymous and Chiastic Parallelism in Tricola in Old Testament Hebrew Psalm Poetry," *Vetus Testamentum* 29: 465–480. Beside the classic studies of Lund in New Testament chiasm, see particularly Thomson, *Chiasmus*.

[2] Explanations of chiasm often begin with the constructs of Hebrew poetry. Cf. Ridderbos and Wolf, "Poetry, Hebrew," 895; Dahood, "Chiasmus," 145.

Chiasm in the Hebrew Bible

For example, Psalm 2, which has parallel lines in nearly every verse,[3] also exhibits chiasm in several places.[4] In verse 1, for instance, although the reflexive parallelism is hidden in English translations by the reordering of the words,[5] in Hebrew the chiastic development is clearly seen:

לָמָּה רָגְשׁוּ גוֹיִם

וּלְאֻמִּים יֶהְגּוּ־רִיק:

The ordering of the synonymous elements of the repetition ("nations" in the first line and "peoples" in the second; "conspire" in the first line and "plot" in the second) is reversed between the two lines so that a basic A B B₁ A₁ form results. A similar chiastic movement occurs in verse 9:

תְּרֹעֵם בְּשֵׁבֶט בַּרְזֶל

כִּכְלִי יוֹצֵר תְּנַפְּצֵם:

The NRSV English translation does not carry the full impact of the chiastic inversion:

> You shall break them with a rod of iron,
> and dash them in pieces like a potter's vessel.

In Hebrew, however, the synonyms found in the second line are in reversed order from their antecedents in the first line. The impact, if translated more literally, would be something like the following:

> You-will-break-them   with-a-rod-of-iron
> Like-a-vessel-of-a-potter you-will-crush-them[6]

---

[3] Cf. Peter C. Craigie, *Psalm 1–50* (Word Biblical Commentary 19; Waco: Word, 1983), 62–65.

[4] Craigie, *Psalm*, 63, identifies chiasms in verses 1, 2, 5, 8, and 10. He seems to overlook another one in verse 9.

[5] In English translations the verse appears to have only simple parallelism:
> "Why do the nations conspire,
>   and the peoples plot in vain?"

[6] La Sor, Hubbard, and Bush, *Old Testament Survey*, 312.

Notice that these simple forms of chiastic development conform to all criteria identified by Thomson:[7]

1. Each shifts at the center of the development as a second line reiterates the ideas of the first.
2. With chiasm on this minimal scale there is no framing that takes place. The unit is simply complete in and of itself within the context of the rest of the poetic development.
3. There are clear parallel elements between the two halves.
4. The referents of the terms at the extremes of the chiastic passage are the same.
5. Each half of the chiastic passage is virtually identical in length to its correspondent half.
6. Because of the simplicity of the development in each of these two examples there is no strong central element; there is, however, a common heightening of the action of the referents in the centrally located verbal forms.

Beyond these simple A B B$_1$ A$_1$ examples there are numerous expressions of more complex chiasms throughout Hebrew poetry. In Isaiah 6:10 the NRSV English version faithfully captures the reverse progression of the lines of the second half of a reflexive poetic development:[8]

הַשְׁמֵן לֵב־הָעָם הַזֶּה	A
וְאָזְנָיו הַכְבֵּד	B
וְעֵינָיו הָשַׁע פֶּן־יִרְאֶה	C
בְעֵינָיו	C$_1$
וּבְאָזְנָיו יִשְׁמָע	B$_1$

---

[7] See 34–35 above.
[8] Cf. Ridderbos and Wolf, "Poetry," 895.

A	Make the mind of this people dull,
B	and stop their ears,
C	and shut their eyes,
C$_1$	so that they may not look with their eyes,
B$_1$	and listen with their ears,
A$_1$	and comprehend with their minds
D	and turn
D$_1$	and be healed.

A_1 וּלְבָבוֹ יָבִין

D   וָשָׁב

D_1 וְרָפָא לוֹ:

Once again, there are multiple elements in reflexive parallelism, and a "tail-piece" that finishes the thought.[9] In each of these examples the repetitions of Hebrew poetry take on a particular reflexive shape that extends the art of parallelism in a more complex direction.[10] Dahood, for example, suggests that chiasm is a form of artistic poetry that gives variety to the language of the Psalms.[11] Ridderbos and Wolf echo that impression when they call chiasm a "means the poets used to escape the peril of monotony in parallelism."[12] Others, as well, refer to chiasm as a means by which to organize poetic thought in order to aid memorization.[13] Whatever its origin or original purpose, chiasm is extensively found throughout the Hebrew Bible.

Chiasm in the New Testament

Yet while the Hebrew Bible contains numerous expressions of chiasm it is the New Testament that more often has been the subject of chiastic investigation.[14] Here again there are many examples of simple reflexive lines in poetic verse. In Romans 10:9–10, for instance, Paul gives this exhortation:[15]

A   ἐὰν ὁμολογήσῃς ἐν τῷ στόματί σου κύριον
    Ἰησοῦν

B   καὶ πιστεύσῃς ἐν τῇ καρδίᾳ σου ὅτι ὁ θεὸς
    αὐτὸν ἤγειρεν ἐκ νεκρῶν, σωθήσῃ:

---

[9] Cf. Thomson's second criterion.

[10] Cf. Cassuto, "Chiastic Word," and "Function."

[11] M. J. Dahood, *Psalms,* Anchor Bible 16 (Garden City, New York: Doubleday, 1965), xxxiii.

[12] Ridderbos and Wolf, "Poetry," 895.

[13] Cf. Thomson, *Chiasmus,* 75.

[14] Lund (*Chiasmus*), Breck (*Shape*), and Thomson (*Chiasmus*) are all New Testament scholars.

[15] Cf. Joachim Jeremias, "Chiasmus in den Paulusbriefen," *Zeitschrift für die neutestamentliche Wissenschaft* 49 (1958): 149, for a similar treatment.

B₁   καρδίᾳ γὰρ πιστεύεται εἰς δικαιοσύνην,
A₁   στόματι δὲ ὁμολογεῖται εἰς σωτηρίαν. [16]

Here the balance is precise and clear. Confessing with the mouth occurs at the beginning of the thought and at the end. More than that, in the first line Paul uses the name "Jesus," which means "saviour," and in the last line he pens the Greek word for "saved." Similarly, in the second and third lines the controlling term is that of believing, with the exact repetition of "in/with the heart" each time. Further, there is conceptual parallelism between the second line (referring to belief in the resurrection of Jesus) and the third line (describing the outcome of this faith, including the repetition of the concept of "salvation" which creates the point of the testimony).[17]

A similar chiastic movement appears to take place in the declaration of I John 3:9:

A   Πᾶς ὁ γεγεννημένος ἐκ τοῦ θεοῦ
B   ἁμαρτίαν οὐ ποιεῖ,
C   ὅτι σπέρμα αὐτοῦ ἐν αὐτῷ μένει,
B₁   καὶ οὐ δύναται ἁμαρτάνειν,
A₁   ὅτι ἐκ τοῦ θεοῦ γεγέννηται. [18]

Once again the repetition of terms and the reflexive paralleling of ideas across the thematic center is readily apparent. The testimony begins and ends by identifying those who "have been born of God" as the subjects under investigation. They "do not sin" (line 2) and "cannot sin" (line 4) because "God's seed abides in them" (line 3). This centered declaration is the hinge upon which the matter of not sinning and the identity of divine genesis turns.

---

[16] A   "...if you confess with your lips that Jesus is Lord
    B   and believe in your heart that God raised him from the dead,
                    you will be saved.
    B₁   For one believes with the heart and so is justified,
    A₁   and one confesses with the mouth and so is saved."
[17] Cf. Blomberg's third, fourth and fifth criteria, 53–54 above.
[18] A   "Those who have been born of God
    B   do not sin,
    C   because God's seed abides in them;
    B₁   they cannot sin,
    A₁   because they have been born of God."

Another example is I John 1:6–7. Here, again, it is relatively simple to observe the chiasm in the movement of the short phrases:[19]

A   Ἐὰν εἴπωμεν ὅτι **κοινωνίαν ἔχομεν** μετ᾽ αὐτοῦ
B   καὶ ἐν τῷ σκότει **περιπατῶμεν**,
C   ψευδόμεθα καὶ οὐ ποιοῦμεν τὴν ἀλήθειαν·
B₁   ἐὰν δὲ ἐν τῷ φωτὶ **περιπατῶμεν** ὡς αὐτός ἐστιν ἐν τῷ φωτί,
A₁   **κοινωνίαν ἔχομεν** μετ᾽ ἀλλήλων...[20]

The argument of the passage flows clearly from A (focused on "fellowship") to B (characterizing the "walk" of the readers) to C (expressing a moral judgement regarding the inner identity) and back again, with the key words in each phrase repeated in their counterpart lines. Repetition of words happens between the reflexive lines of A (**κοινωνίαν ἔχομεν**; "have fellowship") and A₁ (**κοινωνίαν ἔχομεν**, "have fellowship") as well as B (**περιπατῶμεν**, "we are walking") and B1 (**περιπατῶμεν**, "we are walking"). Moreover, the central element holds the significant idea that the writer seeks to convey, holding the halves of the chiasm in creative unity.

Thomson, who, as we saw in Chapter 3, refined the criteria by which to assess micro-chiasm, finds a number of other examples of chiasm scattered throughout the New Testament. One occurs in the passionate exhortation at the beginning of the letter to the Ephesians. Thomson outlines Ephesians 1:4–10 in the following manner, using verse 3 as an introductory frame in line with his second criterion:[21]

---

[19] Key words have been made bold to emphasize the chiastic parallelism.
[20] A   "If we say that we have fellowship with him
    B   while we are walking in darkness,
    C   we lie and do not do what is true;
    B₁   but if we walk in the light as he himself is in the light,
    A₁   we have fellowship with one another..."
[21] Thomson (*Chiasmus*, 27–28) states "Chiasms are sometimes introduced or concluded by a frame passage. Lund himself makes no comment on this, but, judged by examples which he later gives, a 'frame-passage' is a spring-board from which to launch into the chiasmus, or a section which acts as a tail-piece to a chiasmus without itself being part of the chiastic pattern."

Εὐλογητὸς ὁ θεὸς καὶ πατὴρ τοῦ κυρίου ἡμῶν᾽ Ἰησοῦ
Χριστοῦ, ὁ εὐλογήσας ἡμᾶς ἐν πάσῃ εὐλογίᾳ πνευματικῇ
ἐν τοῖς ἐπουρανίοις ἐν Χριστῷ,

A   καθὼς ἐξελέξατο ἡμᾶς ἐν αὐτῷ πρὸ καταβολῆς
         κόσμου εἶναι ἡμᾶς ἁγίους καὶ ἀμώμους
         κατενώπιον αὐτοῦ ἐν ἀγάπῃ,

B   προορίσας ἡμᾶς εἰς υἱοθεσίαν διὰ᾽ Ἰησοῦ
           Χριστοῦ εἰς αὐτόν, κατὰ τὴν **εὐδοκίαν τοῦ**
           θελήματος αὐτοῦ,

C   εἰς ἔπαινον δόξης τῆς χάριτος αὐτοῦ
             ἧς ἐχαρίτωσεν ἡμᾶς ἐν τῷ
             ἠγαπημένῳ.

D   ἐν ᾧ ἔχομεν τὴν ἀπολύτρωσιν
               διὰ τοῦ αἵματος αὐτοῦ, τὴν
               ἄφεσιν τῶν παραπτωμάτων,

C_1 κατὰ τὸ πλοῦτος τῆς χάριτος αὐτοῦ
             ἧς ἐπερίσσευσεν εἰς ἡμᾶς, ἐν πάσῃ
             σοφίᾳ καὶ φρονήσει,

B_1 γνωρίσας ἡμῖν τὸ μυστήριον τοῦ
           θελήματος αὐτοῦ, κατὰ τὴν εὐδοκίαν
           αὐτοῦ

A_1 ἣν προέθετο ἐν αὐτῷ εἰς οἰκονομίαν τοῦ
         πληρώματος τῶν καιρῶν, ἀνακεφαλαιώσασθαι
         τὰ πάντα ἐν τῷ Χριστῷ, τὰ ἐπὶ τοῖς οὐρανοῖς
         καὶ τὰ ἐπὶ τῆς γῆς.[22]

---

[22] "Blessed be the God and Father of our Lord Jesus Christ, who has blessed us in Christ with every spiritual blessing in the heavenly places,

A   just as he chose us in Christ before the foundation of the world to be holy and blameless before him in love.

B   He destined us for adoption as his children through Jesus Christ, according to the good pleasure of his will,

C   to the praise of his glorious grace that he freely bestowed on us in the Beloved.

D   In him we have redemption through his blood, the forgiveness of our trespasses,

C_1 according to the riches of his grace that he lavished on us. With all wisdom and insight

B_1 he has made known to us the mystery of his will, according to his good pleasure

Here, according to Thomson, the gift of redemption, alluded to in the opening setting, becomes prominent in the discourse itself because of its chiastically centered pivotal role (D). Further, there is a clear parallel of both Greek terms and literary themes on either side of this central declaration: gifts are lavished (C/C₁), God's formerly secret will is made known (B/B₁), and the divine intent for the ages actually happens (A/A₁). Beyond this macroscopic chiastic development, Thomson also finds several instances of internal micro-chiasm within specific individual elements of the design of the framework as noted.[23]

Some may argue that Thomson violates his own second rule of chiastic development[24] in this analysis since common exegetical interpretations note the apparent rhetorical flow that seems to continue on through Ephesians 1:14 rather than ending at verse 12.[25] The typical reason for including verses 13–14 in the same literary unit is found in the repeated phrase εἰς ἔπαινον δόξης τῆς χάριτος αὐτοῦ (verses 6, 12, and 14) which seem, to some, to call attention to a thought progression that moves through a series of three forms of salvific activity, each related to human experiences with successive divine persons that constitute the Christian Trinity. Yet, as Barth has shown, verses 11–14 have a somewhat different cadence than the preceding verses, and appear to "mark a transition from objective presentation to personal application."[26] Thus verses 3–10 have their own interior integrity within the context of the larger passage. This allows Thomson to read these verses as a chiastic unit, framed by the introductory praise in verse 3 and its amplification in verses 11–14.

In a similar way, through careful exegetical investigation, Thomson determines that Ephesians 2:11–22,[27] Galatians 5:13–6:2,[28] Colossians 2:6–19,[29] and Romans 5:12–21[30] are intentionally

---

A₁   that he set forth in Christ, as a plan for the fullness of time, to gather up all things in him, things in heaven and things on earth."

[23] Cf. Thomson, *Chiasmus*, 52–53.

[24] Ibid., 27–28: The possibility of a "frame passage" which either introduces or concludes a chiastic passage (or perhaps both), clearly setting the chiasm apart from its larger literary environment.

[25] See Markus Barth, *Ephesians 1–3* (Anchor Bible 34; Garden City, New York: Doubleday, 1974), 97–101.

[26] Ibid., 98.

[27] Thomson, *Chiasmus*, 84–115.

[28] Ibid., 116–151.

[29] Ibid., 152–185.

[30] Ibid., 186–212.

chiastically designed by Paul. Reflecting on the incidence of chiasm in the New Testament, he makes the following observation:

> ...it may be that chiasmus did not have a single or a simple function, but was, in general terms, a *tool of rhetorical composition*, capable of functioning as an art form, an *aide-memoire*, acting as a structuring device as a consequence of its presence, while enhancing in a clear, yet flexible way... the impact of the argument.[31]

His study views Galatians 5:13–6:2 as a case in point.[32] Using the inductive clue of two Pauline lists of human behaviour or character (5:19–21a and 5:22–23a) separated by a stern warning, he begins looking for a simple ABA pattern. Moving outward at either end he finds the pairing of declarations related to, first, the limits set by the law, second, the works of the flesh, third, life in the Spirit, and finally, care for one another. Comparing the internal elements of each of these phrases, including repetition of words and ideas, he begins to explore the extended possibilities of chiasm. His investigation reveals the following:

A   Ὑμεῖς γὰρ ἐπ' ἐλευθερίᾳ ἐκλήθητε, ἀδελφοί· μόνον μὴ τὴν ἐλευθερίαν εἰς ἀφορμὴν τῇ σαρκί, ἀλλὰ διὰ τῆς ἀγάπης δουλεύετε ἀλλήλοις. ὁ γὰρ πᾶς *νόμος* ἐν ἑνὶ λόγῳ πεπλήρωται, ἐν τῷ·' Ἀγαπήσεις τὸν πλησίον σου ὡς σεαυτόν.

B   εἰ δὲ ἀλλήλους δάκνετε καὶ κατεσθίετε, βλέπετε μὴ ὑπ' ἀλλήλων ἀναλωθῆτε.

C   Λέγω δέ, **πνεύματι** περιπατεῖτε καὶ ἐπιθυμίαν σαρκὸς οὐ μὴ τελέσητε.

D   ἡ γὰρ σὰρξ ἐπιθυμεῖ κατὰ τοῦ πνεύματος, τὸ δὲ πνεῦμα κατὰ τῆς σαρκός, ταῦτα γὰρ ἀλλήλοις ἀντίκειται, ἵνα μὴ ἃ ἐὰν θέλητε ταῦτα ποιῆτε.

E   εἰ δὲ **πνεύματι** ἄγεσθε, **οὐκ** ἐστὲ ὑπὸ *νόμον*.

---

[31] Ibid., 223.
[32] Ibid., 116–151.

F
                          φανερὰ δέ ἐστιν τὰ ἔργα
                          τῆς σαρκός, ἅτινά ἐστιν
                          πορνεία, ἀκαθαρσία,
                          ἀσέλγεια, εἰδωλολατρία,
                          φαρμακεία, ἔχθραι, ἔρις,
                          ζῆλος, θυμοί, ἐριθεῖαι,
                          διχοστασίαι, αἱρέσεις,
                          φθόνοι, μέθαι, κῶμοι καὶ
                          τὰ ὅμοια τούτοις,

G
                                    ἃ προλέγω ὑμῖν
                                  καθὼς προεῖπον ὅτι οἱ
                                  τὰ τοιαῦτα
                                  πράσσοντες
                                  βασιλείαν θεοῦ οὐ
                                  κληρονομήσουσιν.

F_1
                          Ὁ δὲ καρπὸς τοῦ
                          πνεύματός ἐστιν ἀγάπη
                          χαρὰ εἰρήνη, μακροθυμία,
                          χρηστότης ἀγαθωσύνη,
                          πίστις πραΰτης ἐγκράτεια·

E_1
                    κατὰ τῶν τοιούτων οὐκ ἔστιν
                    νόμος.

D_1
                οἱ δὲ τοῦ Χριστοῦ [Ἰησοῦ] τὴν σάρκα
                ἐσταύρωσαν σὺν τοῖς παθήμασιν καὶ
                ταῖς ἐπιθυμίαις.

C_1
            εἰ ζῶμεν **πνεύματι, πνεύματι** καὶ
            στοιχῶμεν.

B_1
       μὴ γινώμεθα κενόδοξοι, ἀλλήλους
       προκαλούμενοι, ἀλλήλοις φθονοῦντες.

A_1
  Ἀδελφοί, ἐὰν καὶ προλημφθῇ ἄνθρωπος ἔν τινι
παραπτώματι, ὑμεῖς οἱ πνευματικοὶ καταρτίζετε τὸν
τοιοῦτον ἐν πνεύματι πραΰτητος, σκοπῶν σεαυτόν μὴ

καὶ σὺ πειρασθῇς. Ἀλλήλων τὰ βάρη βαστάζετε καὶ
οὕτως ἀναπληρώσετε τὸν *νόμον* τοῦ Χριστοῦ.[33]

---

[33] A   For you were called to freedom, brothers and sisters; only do not use your freedom as an opportunity for self-indulgence, but through love become slaves to one another. For the whole law is summed up in a single commandment, "you shall love your neighbor as yourself."

B   If, however, you bite and devour one another, take care that you are not consumed by one another.

C   Live by the Spirit, I say, and do not gratify the desires of the flesh.

D   For what the flesh desires is opposed to the Spirit, and what the Spirit desires is opposed to the flesh; for these are opposed to each other, to prevent you from doing what you want.

E   But if you are led by the Spirit, you are not subject to the law.

F   Now the works of the flesh are obvious: fornication, impurity, licentiousness, idolatry, sorcery, enmities, strife, jealousy, anger, quarrels, dissensions, factions, envy, drunkenness, carousing, and things like these.

G   I am warning you, as I warned you before: those who do such things will not inherit the kingdom of God.

F_1 By contrast, the fruit of the Spirit is love, joy peace, patience, kindness, generosity, faithfulness, gentleness, and self-control.

E_1 There is no law against such things.

D_1 And those who belong to Christ Jesus have crucified the flesh with its passions and desires.

C_1 If we live by the Spirit, let us also be guided by the Spirit.

B_1 Let us not become conceited, competing against one another, envying one another.

Once again, all six of Thomson's criteria for micro-chiasm are clearly evident in this passage:

1. There is a shift in emphasis at the center, as the primary focus on evils related to "the works of the flesh" (F) give way to a celebration of "the fruit of the Spirit" (F_1) in the context of a warning that separates those who practice the former from those who exhibit the latter (G).
2. In this instance of chiastic development there is no specific "frame passage" or "tail-piece"; rather the passage exists as a single unit in a larger discussion of the nature and character of community life.
3. There are clear parallels between elements of the first half and those of the second half of the passage.[34]
4. The exhortation toward behaviour modification occurs at both extremes (A and A_1), as well as at the center (G).
5. There is similarity in length of each half,[35] as well as between corresponding parts within each half.[36]
6. The central element summarizes the intent of the passage as a whole: works of the flesh are inconsistent with life in the kingdom.

In this and other analyses of New Testament passages Thomson demonstrates his thesis that chiastic development is apparent throughout the New Testament, and that it functions as a literary device according to certain rules. These rules become the criteria by which other suspected chiastic developments must be judged.

Thomson's work is intriguing in several ways. For one thing, although he believes strongly that there must be clear verbal parallels and correspondence between the halves of the chiasm as a safeguard

---

A_1 My friends, if anyone is detected in a transgression, you who have received the Spirit should restore such a one in a spirit of gentleness. Take care that you yourselves are not tempted. Bear one another's burdens, and in this way you will fulfil the law of Christ.

[34] E.g. οὐκ ἐστὲ ὑπὸ νόμον ("you are not subject to the law") in E and κατὰ τῶν τοιούτων οὐκ ἐστιν νόμος ("There is no law against such things") in E_1; πνεύματι περιπατεῖτε ("live by the Spirit") in C and ζῶμεν πνεύματι ("live by the Spirit") in C_1; the paralleled lists in F and F_1.

[35] 117 words in A–F and 82 in F_1–A_1.

[36] A (36), A_1 (34); B (11), B_1 (7); C (10), C_1 (6); D (24), D_1 (14); E (8), E_1 (6); F (28), F_1 (13).

against what he deems eisegetically imposed structures of supposed "thematic" chiasm,[37] his chiastic examples often have few exact corresponding verbal parallels between halves, and are, in fact, based in significant part on thematic correspondence. The "works of the flesh" are not identical with the "fruit of the Spirit" in Galatians 5, although the correspondence between the terms and the lists creates a delightful chiastic symmetry. In this regard Thomson overstates his objections against Lund, Clark, and others who see symmetry in thematic elements of passages. If Thomson were to rely only on direct verbal parallels between corresponding elements in each half of his Ephesians 1 chiasm he would find his research working against his premise.

Secondly, Thomson has taken his chiastic investigations well beyond the limited scope of the obvious reflexive parallels found in four to six lines of Hebrew poetry. In doing so he has shown chiastic movement that functions in passages of much greater length than in its most common or most easily perceived micro-chiastic form. Although Thomson himself does not believe chiasm works on passages longer than about 15 lines,[38] he appears to stretch his own concept of chiasm well beyond the limits it seems to have had when it functioned in its earliest Hebrew poetic forms.[39]

This leads us to a further investigation of the relationship between micro-chiasm and macro-chiasm. How do they function alike? In what manner are they dissimilar? Is there a chiastic manner of thinking that initially gave shape to the reflexive parallelism found in lines of poetry, but which also functions in the macro-chiastic development of narrative themes and extended discourse?

It is to these matters we turn in the next chapter.

---

[37] Thomson, *Chiasmus*, 27–29.

[38] Thomson, *Chiasmus*, 29–30.

[39] Ridderbos and Wolf, "Poetry," 895.

CHAPTER 5

BEYOND MICRO-CHIASM
TO MACRO-CHIASM

From Poetic Reflexivity to Narrative Art

It is apparent from the examples of chiasm surveyed in Chapter 4 that as the length of a chiastically developed passage increases and the number of literary sub-units that serve as its building blocks multiply, the immediate clarity of the chiasm is often reduced. Rather than expressing a tight and direct balance of words and phrases across a pivotal center for poetic impact, longer passages (especially when the genre is narrative rather than poetry) often contain elements that are not in word-for-word parallel with their reflexive counterparts and sometimes hold a more thematic correspondence with other elements of the passage.

It is at this point that two streams of scholarly reflection diverge. Some, like Thomson (despite the length of some of his own examples as noted in Chapter 4), believe that chiasm only functions on a micro-chiastic level,[1] while others, such as Blomberg, find ample evidence of the use of macro-chiasm throughout biblical literature. At the heart of the discussion is the question of the character of correspondence between parallel terms or units. What is the point behind chiasm? Why did it originate in the first place? What was the desired effect in reflexive parallel communication techniques?

---

[1] Thomson, *Chiasmus*, 29–30; cf. Porter and Reed, "Philippians as a Macro-Chiasm," 221.

Origins of Chiasm

Although there is no treatise on chiasm in the literature of antiquity, some scholars have speculated on the manner in which chiasm functioned in preliterate societies, as well as the function of chiastic development on several levels in literate cultures of antiquity. Probing these hypotheses may prove helpful in finding some understanding of the relationship between micro-chiasm and macro-chiasm.

From his experiences while growing up in and later studying the communication habits of several cultures in the Mediterranean world, Bailey suggests that chiasm has its roots in the storytelling practices of pre-literate cultures. Bailey has engaged in extensive research into methods of storytelling and formal instruction, particularly in communities of low and moderate literacy rates. He finds chiasm still in common expression in the communication patterns of orally attuned societies of the modern Middle East. Further, in comparing ancient narratives with similar expressions in contemporary society he found comparable conventions of storytelling.[2]

Bailey believes that chiasm naturally evolved among peoples who transmitted identity and history through repeated ballads and heroic tales. He claims that oral recitations are often governed by what he calls the "inversion principle." This is the tendency, according to Bailey, which moves an oral narrative in a path that brings the tale to a climax in the middle, and then returns the events to a status quo that resembles life and situations as they were described near the beginning of the story. There is, in such storytelling, according to Bailey, a tendency to come full circle in thought processes from beginning to end.[3]

Bailey offers a number of reasons why this is the case.[4] First, chiastic inversion (repetition of terms and ideas across a midpoint) and *inclusio* (returning to an original expression or its variation to bring a tale to completion) aids in memorization.[5] With its balance of related words, themes, and sentence structure chiasm offers a way to organize and connect the elements of a prose or poetic recitation.[6] Where details

---

[2] Bailey, *Poet & Peasant*, 28–37.

[3] Bailey, *Poet & Peasant*, 49.

[4] Ibid., 30–37. See also Thomson, *Chiasmus*, 30–35.

[5] Bailey, *Poet & Peasant*, 31–32; Thomson, *Chiasmus*, 75.

[6] Bailey, *Poet & Peasant*, 35; Thomson, 30–35.

of a story must be carried along from generation to generation in the mind rather than on paper, this becomes very important.[7]

Second, chiastically developed thought is primarily inductive rather than deductive.[8] No "thesis" is stated at the beginning, to be aided and supported by syllogistic logic. Instead, the "point" of the narrative approaches by way of steps of measured anticipation.

Third, there is inherent artistic beauty to chiastically ordered communication.[9] The skill of the storyteller is at stake. Both a well-told story and the apparent sagacity of its teller are a product of practice and repetition. This aspect supports the observations of Dahood that chiasm is a form of poetic artistry that gives variety to the language of the Psalms.[10]

If Bailey is correct (and unfortunately there has been little research either to confirm or deny his hypotheses in this area), the purpose of chiasm in communication is not limited to the playful and artistic reflexive parallelism in several lines of poetry. Chiasm, then, might also be considered a general pattern of thought processes in which the elements of a narrative might be arranged as easily in a reflexive parallel composition as we tend to think of linear arguments developed either deductively or inductively.

Given this perspective on the purpose and function of chiasm, the distinction between micro-chiasm and macro-chiasm is useful only as a way in which to differentiate the length of chiastic developments. Some consist primarily in direct verbal parallels and are primarily found in a few short lines of poetry; these are identified as micro-chiasm. Longer passages that develop repeated themes in a reflexive manner, inversely stated on either side of the midpoint of the passage are called macro-chiasms. Because of this, Thomson's criteria for assessing chiasm are sufficient for the rapid interchange of micro-

---

[7] Bailey gives numerous examples in *Through Peasant Eyes* (Grand Rapids: Eerdmans, 1980) of parables of Jesus in which he finds chiastic development. He believes that this arises from the techniques of storytelling present in Jesus' culture and was aided by the oral tradition that carried the teachings of Jesus before they were written down (xiv–xx).

[8] Bailey, *Poet & Peasant*, 74–75; Thomson, 35, refers to this as a type of "structuring device" in a *lectuo continua* or *scriptio continua* communication frame of reference.

[9] Bailey, *Poet & Peasant*, 75, note 54; Cf. Thomson, *Chiasmus*, 34; Ridderbos and Wolf, "Poetry," 895.

[10] Dahood, *Psalms*, xxxiii.

chiasm and its direct verbal correspondences between lines or short sections.

Yet the whole range of chiastic reflexivity is not contained in micro-chiastic expressions, if, indeed, narrative chiasm is a tool by which to craft tales and then to commit them to memory for successive recountings. At this level of expanded chiastic reflexivity, where structural and conceptual patterns are paired and reversed, Blomberg's broader understanding of and criteria for macro-chiastic developments (coupled, as they often are, with direct verbal pairings), is also necessary, as is the criteria by which he proposes that such passages be tested.

Blomberg's criteria prove useful, for instance, in assessing Breck's appraisal of Matthew 3:1–4:17. Breck believes that this passage was developed from "two originally independent units (3:1–17; 4:1–17) worked together into a chiastic pattern,"[11] and he relies on thematic correspondence rather than verbal parallels in the chiastic movement he identifies:

A (3:1f): John's message—"Repent, for the Kingdom of heaven
                    is at hand."
B   (3:3): Isaiah's prophecy concerning John.
C   (3:4–6): John in the wilderness.
D   (3:7–10): Pharisees and Sadducees come to
                              be baptized.
E   (3:11ab): Jesus is mightier than John.
F   (3:11c): "He will baptize you
                                          with the Holy Spirit and
                                          with fire."
E_1 (3:12): Jesus will execute final
                                     judgement.
D_1 (3:13–17): Jesus comes to be baptized.
C_1 (4:1–11): Jesus in the wilderness.
B_1 (4:12–16): Isaiah's prophecy concerning Jesus.
A_1 (4:17): Jesus' message—"Repent, for the Kingdom of
                    heaven is at hand."

There are, indeed, a number of literary cues that lend support to Breck's chiastic interpretation of this passage. First, Matthew draws on both the continuity and discontinuity between John and Jesus in terms

---

[11] Breck, *Shape*, 125.

of message and personal style; thus Breck's sense of chiasm developed along the lines of a comparison between these figures is possible.[12] Second, the fulfilment of prophecies from the book of Isaiah fits the chiastic pattern Breck describes.[13] Third, 3:1 and 4:17 form an effective *inclusio* binding the flow of the narrative together and setting these scenes off from those that precede as well as those that follow. Fourth, John's announcement about Jesus' unique character and mission is clearly the testimonial highlight of the passage, and thus belongs at center stage. In other words, the heightened significance of the pivotal element in the chiastic structure fits well with the declarations as developed in the gospel at this point.

At the same time, when measured by Blomberg's criteria for macro-chiasm, Breck's analysis leaves many gaps. For one thing, the temptation of Jesus in the wilderness (4:1–11) is hardly parallel to John's chosen wilderness lifestyle (3:4–6). When Breck identifies these sections as similar in theme or content he ignores the general consensus of scholarship that views it otherwise, violating Blomberg's second criterion. Jesus enters the wilderness as a place alien and foreign, while John makes the wilderness his home. John thrives on the substance of the wilderness while Jesus endures the threat of the wilderness. Not only that, but both the length of these passages and the actual terminology used in each are very different, thus working against Blomberg's third and fourth criteria. "John in the wilderness" comprises three verses of locative description while "Jesus in the wilderness" is eleven verses of dialogue and action.

Again, the interaction between John and the Pharisees and Sadducees who come seeking baptism (3:7–10) is dissimilar to that between John and Jesus at his baptism (3:13–17) in tone, wording, and overall intent. John is antagonistic toward the Pharisees and Sadducees but subservient toward Jesus; the coming of the Pharisees and the Sadducees to John results in a diatribe against them, which comprises nearly the entire section, identified by Breck, while the baptism of Jesus includes short dialogues and a number of character movements

---

[12] Cf. Robert H. Gundry, *Matthew: A Commentary on His Literary and Theological Art* (Grand Rapids: Eerdmans, 1982), 42–43.

[13] For John the prophecy of Isaiah stands as the lead element in his story, serving as an evaluation of what his ministry would be; for Jesus, a similar prophecy from Isaiah is used as a summation of things he has previously accomplished. Chiastically these reviews thus stand near the extremes of the larger narrative.

and actions. Jesus' baptism becomes, within the passage, a consecration for divine service, while the occasion of the arrival of the Pharisees and Sadducees plays to the rejection theme woven throughout the gospel.[14]

These matters of exegesis certainly diminish the need to read the passage in chiastic terms, and limit the strength of a "centered" passage to hold or summarise the meaning of the whole (Blomberg's eighth criterion). More than that, they point to the need for clear criteria by which to interpret the nature of the correspondence between paralleled elements of passages where macro-chiasm is suspected, but where the clear correspondence of repeated terms or phrases is absent.

This is particularly important in the ongoing quest for chiasm, especially in longer passages of both the Hebrew Bible and the New Testament. Watts, for example, believes that the collected prophecies of Isaiah are redacted chiastically.[15] Scott[16] and Breck[17] analyse the entire gospel of Mark and find it chiastically structured. The Fourth Gospel is another prominent target of sweeping chiastic investigation, with a variety of interpreters finding chiastic designs to the very limits of its pages.[18] Like Lund's analysis seeking intentional chiasm in the design of Paul's extended "spiritual gifts" discourse of I Corinthians 12–14,[19] most of these expansive findings are not universally recognised. While each of these passages may contain elements of repetition across a prominent center, the multiple literary panels that form the substance of each, together with their prosaic flow, detract from a sense of chiastic clarity and precision. It takes strong literary glue to hold lengthy narratives together in true chiastic form.

Testing the Criteria

Still, as many have shown, the glue is not impossible to find. Bailey, for instance, suggests chiastic development in the story of

---

[14] Cf. Jack Dean Kingsbury, *Matthew: Structure, Christology, Kingdom* (Philadelphia: Fortress, 1975), 165–166.

[15] John D. W. Watts, *Isaiah 1–33* (Waco, Texas: Word, 1985), l–liv.

[16] M. Philip Scott, "Chiastic Structure: A Key to the Interpretation of Mark's Gospel," *Biblical Theology Bulletin* 15 (1985): 17–26.

[17] Breck, *Shape*, 144–173.

[18] So Ellis, *Genius*; Bruno Barnhart, *The Good Wine: Reading from the Center* (New York: Paulist Press, 1993); Breck, *Shape*, 191–197.

[19] Lund, *Chiasmus*, 164.

Shadrach, Meshach and Abednego facing Nebuchadnezzar's torturous furnace in Daniel 3:13–30.[20] His analysis is as follows:

A   The king in anger commands that SMA [Shadrach, Meshach, Abednego] be brought in

B   Serve my God or you will be punished
Who is the God who will deliver you

C   The God we serve will deliver us from the king
We will not serve or worship the golden image

D   The fire is heated seven times

E   The king orders SMA bound and cast into the fire
SMA are bound and cast into the fire

F   The king asks about three men bound in the fire
The king sees four men loose in the fire, one like a son of man

E_1 The king orders SMA to come out
SMA come out

D_1 The fire did not touch them

C_1 The God of SMA delivered his servants from the king
They did not serve or worship any God except God

B_1 Speak against the God of SMA and you will be punished
There is no other god who can deliver in this way

A_1 The king promotes SMA in Babylon

Here the movement of the story, as Bailey outlines it, follows a reflexive pattern, and even elements of the speeches and narrative descriptions parallel one another across the midpoint of the tale. The intended impact of the story occurs neither at the beginning nor at the

---

[20] Lund, *Chiasmus*, 51.

close of the narrative. Rather, it happens at the heart, in element F, where the destruction intended for the defiant trio is miraculously averted, and their saviour appears with them in the fire.

When Bailey's chiastic hypothesis regarding this story is tested against Blomberg's criteria for assessing chiastic development it appears to be sustained. The first criterion is that the structure of the passage has no better explanation. As Goldingay notes, scholars have generally recognized a reflexive development in this narrative.[21] Furthermore, the overall development of the second half follows a clearly inverse pattern to that of the first half. Third, there are clear examples of parallel elements between the halves (the summary themes noted by Bailey echo the great correspondence in actual repetition of terms and phrases within the narrative). Fourth, the repetition of words and phrases carry the central meaning of the narrative.[22] Fifth, the language of Daniel 3, though similar to the rest of the book, has its own vocabulary. Sixth, Bailey's outline shows the multiple pairings that take place in the overall development of the tale. Seven, the movements from section to section reflect exactly the broadly perceived natural breaks in the passage. Eighth, the central element of the chiasm is, indeed, the central element of the story—Shadrach, Meshach, and Abednego are spared in the fire even as a divine apparition startles Nebuchadnezzar. Finally, there are no unusual, displaced, or missing elements in this chiastic outline of the passage; all the pieces fit.

When Bailey turns to the New Testament, he finds a similar chiastic development in Jesus' dialogue with the wealthy ruler on the topic of riches and obedience in Luke 18:18–30. Once again, according to Bailey, the narrative doubles back upon itself after reaching a climactic point of meaning at its central element. In his reading of the pericope, the chiastic flow unfolds in this manner (Bailey's summary notations appear on the right side):[23]

1	A certain ruler asked him,	ETERNAL LIFE
	"Good teacher, what having done I shall inherit *eternal life?*"	

---

[21] John E. Goldingay, *Daniel* (Word Biblical Commentary 30; Dallas: Word, 1989), 68–69.

[22] Goldingay (ibid., 68) states: "This [the oral background to the tale] is reflected in the extensive use of repetition…" Goldingay then lists eight repeated phrases, showing also how some reverse order from the initial expression to the later expression.

[23] Bailey, *Poet and Peasant*, 52–53.

2   And Jesus said to him,
       "Why do you call me good?
       No one is good but one, even God.
       You know the commandments:
        Do not commit adultery 7 (loyalty to family)

                                     THE
       Do not kill   6   OLD
                                     OBEDIENCE
       Do not steal   8 (property) —fulfilled
       Do not bear false witness   9
       Honor your father and mother." 5 (loyalty to parents)
       And he said,
       "All of these I have observed from my youth."
3   And hearing Jesus said to him,
       "One thing you still lack.
       Sell everything you have THE NEW OBEDIENCE
       and distribute to the poor —demanded (the ruler)
       and you will have treasure in heaven
       and come and follow me."
        4   And hearing this   NEW OBEDIENCE
          he became deeply grieved   —too hard
          for he was very rich.
           5   And seeing him Jesus said,
              "How hard it is
              for those who have possessions
                             ENTER THE
            to enter the kingdom of God.
                               KINGDOM
            It is easier for a camel to go through a
            needle's eye
              than for a rich man
              to enter the kingdom of God."
       4¹   And those who heard said,   NEW
                                   OBEDIENCE
        "And who is able to be saved?" —too hard
        But he said, "What is impossible with men -
                           possible only
           is possible with God."
                           with God
3¹   And Peter said,   THE NEW OBEDIENCE

"Lo, we have *left everything we possess* —fulfilled
(disciples)
and *followed you.* "
2^1 And he said to them,
"Truly I say to you
there is no one who has left
house   (property)   NEW OBEDIENCE
or wife   (loyalty to family)—fulfilled (any man)
or brothers (loyalty to family)
or parents   (loyalty to parents)
or children (loyalty to family)
for the sake of the kingdom
1^1 who will not receive much more in this time   ETERNAL LIFE
and in the age to come–*eternal life.* "

Once again Bailey shows how the narrative, in his particular reading of its development, leads to a climax at the midpoint. Also, the elements of the tale, as they appear on either side of the midpoint, have a parallel quality about them (Blomberg's criteria two through seven). The question of eternal life is broached at the beginning and at the end. A code of conduct is elucidated near the beginning and once again near the end. The nature of wealth and its impact on religious devotion are explored in common locations from the midpoint. Of course, at the heart of it all is the main teaching (Blomberg's criterion eight). It is not eternal life as a desired end in and of itself that is the key to happiness, but rather the process of entering the kingdom of God (which then leads to eternal life). Whatever "eternal life" might be about must be found by way of entering the kingdom of God (the two are not necessarily synonymous). And whatever entering the kingdom of God is about is not accomplished either with wealth or obedience as understood in the "old" frame of reference.

There appear to be no "ruptures" in this exploration of the text (Blomberg's criterion nine). Still, the primary issue that needs to be addressed as Bailey posits his reading of Luke 18:18–30 is Blomberg's first criterion for macro-chiasm: is there a problem in understanding the development of the text in other readings? Indeed, as Nolland has shown, the form of the dialogue "has caused some to dispute the original unity of the pericope."[24] The interaction between Jesus and the

---

[24] John Nolland, *Luke 9:21–18:34* (Word Biblical Commentary 35b; Dallas: Word, 1993), 884.

ruler, coupled with the intrusion of the question from Peter, seems staged and artificial. Because of this many scholars attempt to find the Markan material and separate it from the Lukan material, and then comment on the form of the interaction in the Markan version.[25] No satisfactory literary analysis has been put forward except for the chiastic arrangement developed by Bailey.

It seems, therefore, that Blomberg's criteria are helpful, and that chiastic development in a number of biblical texts is both likely and an essential part of understanding the manner in which these texts focus the impact of their content.

Extending the Reach

Before moving on to the Johannine farewell discourse there remains one further exploration. What is the length to which a passage may exhibit chiastic development? The Johannine farewell discourse, after all, comprises five chapters. Is it even conceivable that a passage of such length may find its best interpretation through a chiastic reading?

There are a number of passages at various locations the Hebrew Bible that give evidence of chiastic flow over a rather lengthy narrative development.

Ehud the Judge (Judges 3:12–30)

A clear expression of chiasm is found in the book of Judges. One of the earliest stories of a hero recounted in Israel's history concerns the daring exploit of Ehud.[26] This tale, recounted in Judges 3:12–30, is taut and economical in its delivery, making great use of

---

[25] Ibid. 884–885.

[26] For an extended and intriguing analysis of the Ehud story in its historical environment see Baruch Halpern, *The First Historians: The Hebrew Bible and History* (San Francisco: Harper & Row, 1988), 39–68.

word play and irony.[27] More importantly, it appears to be carefully crafted in the reflexive movements of chiastic structure:[28]

A   Moab is made strong over the Israelites. (English
                      translation 3:12)
B   Moab strikes down Israel. (3:13–14)
C   Israel sends Ehud with tribute to Eglon. (3:15–17)
D   At the "idols" marking conquered territory Ehud
                      sends his fellow Israelites home. (3:18)
E   Ehud returns to Eglon. (3:19a)
F   Eglon's attendants leave (to allow for a secret
                      message). (3:19b)
G   Ehud enters Eglon's private quarters. (3:20)
H   Ehud draws his sword. (3:21a)
I   Ehud thrusts his word into Eglon's
                      belly.(3:21b)
H_1 Ehud does not withdraw his sword. (3:22)
G_1 Ehud leaves Eglon's private quarters. (3:23)
F_1 Eglon's attendants re-enter (the message
                      remains secret). (3:24–25)
E_1 Ehud gets away from Eglon's house. (3:26a)
D_1 At the "idols" marking conquered territory Ehud
                      escapes and summons the Israelites. (3:26b–27)
C_1 Ehud leads Israel in attack on the Moabites. (3:28)
B_1 Israel strikes down Moab. (3:29)
A_1 Moab is made subject to the Israelites. (3:30)

The presence of this pattern is confirmed by a close analysis of the Hebrew text. At the center of the story is a clear wordplay using three terms—יצא (to go out), בוא (to go in), and סגר (to close/shut). They move the action back and forth quickly in the central section:

---

[27] Ehud is a left-handed man from the tribe of Benjamin (which means, "son of my right hand"); King Eglon believes he is receiving tribute but instead he is forced to "eat" their retribution; the sword of Ehud, prominent in nearly all the important action, remains concealed throughout–first under the coat of Ehud and then in the belly of Eglon; Eglon's servant think their master has locked himself in for privacy while in fact Ehud has locked them out for privacy of a different kind.

[28] Although the outline that follows is mine, the reflexive elements are suggested by others, including, e.g., Robert G. Boling, *Judges* (Anchor Bible 6A; Garden City, New York: Doubleday, 1975), 85–87.

- Eglon's servants go out (יצא)   *verse 19*
- Ehud enters (בוא)   *verse 20*
- Ehud's sword enters (בוא)   *verse 22*
- Eglon's belly closes (סגר)   *verse 22*
- Ehud's sword comes out the other side (יצא)   *verse 22*
- Ehud goes out (יצא)   *verse 23*
- Ehud closes the doors (סגר)   *verse 23*
- Ehud goes out (יצא)   *verse 24*
- Eglon's servants enter (בוא)   *verse 24*

It is obvious that some careful crafting went into the telling of this story so that even these word plays add a movement similar to the duelling thrusts of fencers, back and forth on the floor of contest. It appears that the chiasm of the narrative is intrinsic to the method in which the story was crafted. It might have been told in other ways, as other stories within the book of Judges were. For instance, it might have been developed through a linear progression focusing on the battles that ultimately lead to Israel's victory over Moab. Similarly, the emphasis could have been on a hero-characterization depicting more of the personal qualities of Ehud and the circumstances that brought him to leadership in the first place. Again, the author had the opportunity to focus on the contrasting riches of each nation and the strengths of their peoples. Each of these storytelling methods is used in other literary segments throughout the book of Judges.[29] However, in this particular episode, the story itself is chiastically recounted, so that the form of the story appears to be as important as the substance it conveys.

Applying Blomberg's criteria to this reading of the Ehud tale there is, again, confirmation of macro-chiastic development. Elements of the story, such as the references to the "stones" in verses 19 and 26,[30] have long puzzled interpreters (criterion one), as has the rapid movement of segments of the story while other parts seem to be told

---

[29] For example, the story of Othniel (Judges 3:7–11) focuses in a linear manner only on the battles and subsequent victory; the tale of Deborah and Barak (Judges 4–5) hardly notices either the plight of the people or the processes of battles and conquest, focusing almost entirely upon the character of the heroic figures who stand above the people; the story of Gideon (Judges 6–8) expends much energy on defining the strength or weakness of the combatant forces, including the numbers of soldiers and the fighting equipment available to each army.

[30] Boling, *Judges*, 86.

with laborious detail.[31] There are multiple sets (criterion six) of clear examples of parallelism between the halves (criterion two), including both verbal and conceptual correspondence (criterion three) that call attention to themselves in the dominant images and terms of the passage (criteria four and five). The outline of the chiastic narrative development is consistent (criterion nine) and follows the natural movement and breaks in the text (criterion seven). The center of the chiasm delivers the message proclaimed by the passage as a whole— judgement on Eglon (criterion eight).

The Flood Story (Genesis 6:10–9:19)

Another more lengthy example of chiastic development is found in the story of the flood in Genesis 6:10–9:19.[32] There are consistent and obvious elements that mark the movement of the temporal details of the story in paired steps on either side of the central element.[33] These elements of plot are stated in such a way that, along with the repetition of words and phrases, there is also a dramatic development that builds between parallel ideas:[34]

A   The significance of Noah (6:9)
B   Sons of Noah: Shem, Ham, and Japheth (6:10)
C   God sees the character of flesh on earth (6:11–12)
D   Promise of global destruction (6:13)
E   Design of the instrument for salvation (ark)
                                                                        (6:14–16)
F   Covenant of life through death (6:17–21)

---

[31] Ibid, 85–87.

[32] Cf., for similar structural analysis, B. W. Anderson, "From Analysis to Synthesis: The Interpretation of Gen 1–11," *Journal of Biblical Literature* 97 (1978): 23–39; Gordon J. Wenham, *Genesis 1–15* (Word Biblical Commentary 1; Waco: Word, 1987), 155–158.

[33] Note the balance of parallel themes that mark the progress of the story in ascendancy as it unfolds, and in decendancy as the tale moves to its conclusion.

[34] Note the following movement of themes: there is initially an unsettled foreboding of a world run rampant with evil; this gives rise to premonitions and then promises of judgement, which are then brought to resolution through the crisis of the flood, which restores the world to its creational character of peace and harmony.

G	Noah's response to God (6:22)
H	Command to enter the ark as righteous people (7:1–5)
I	Noah and all entrusted to him enter the ark (7:6–10)
J	The passengers in the ark during the days of the rain (7:11–16)
K	Rising waters (7:17–18)
L	Ark carried above engulfed mountains (7:19–20)
M	Breath of God removed, causing death (7:21–24)
N	God remembers Noah and those with him in the ark (8:1)
M_1	Breath of God blows, removing death (8:2–3)
L_1	Ark rests on exposed mountains (8:4–5)
K_1	Subsiding waters (8:6–12)
J_1	The passengers in the ark during the days of the drying (8:13–17)
I_1	Noah and all entrusted to him leave the ark (8:18–22)
H_1	Command to enter the earth as righteous people (9:1–7)
G_1	Noah's response to God (9:8)
F_1	Covenant of life through death (9:9–13)
E_1	Design of the instrument for salvation (bow) (9:14–15a)
D_1	Promise of no more global destruction (9:15b)
C_1	God sees the character of flesh on earth (9:16–17)
B_1	Sons of Noah: Shem, Ham, and Japheth (9:18)
A_1	The significance of Noah (9:19)

The story begins with Noah and the status of his family, progresses by stages through the divine assessment of earth's moral crisis and God's response, and the affairs of the Ark. Once the remembrance of 8:1 is noted, the narrative returns again on the path it followed in the first half of the story, only now in reverse order.

In assessing this chiastic reading of Genesis 6:10–9:19 it is important to note the following:

1. There is clearly a repetition of both words and terms from the first half of the passage to the second half (Blomberg's criteria two through four).[35]
2. Other scholars identify the divisions of the text as expressed (Blomberg's criterion one).[36]
3. There is balance between the halves of the passage so that there is similarity in length, structure, and content, supported by clear repetitions of words or ideas (Blomberg's criteria five and six).
4. The center element, Genesis 8:1, provides a key thought by which the rest of the passages is to be interpreted (Blomberg's criterion eight). Even though God is willing to allow the features and creatures of earth to be removed from the face of the planet (in effect, allowing them to be forgotten, since, in Genesis 1–2 things gain identity through *naming*; when their names are no longer remembered they will cease to exist), he remembers Noah, and in the remembering saves his life and the lives with him.
5. In the book of Genesis, shaped by the ten "genealogies", Genesis 6:9–9:19 forms a complete literary unit (Blomberg's criterion seven).[37]
6. Genesis 8:1 functions as a climax without any clear parallels in the passage as a whole (Blomberg's criterion eight).
7. The flow of the outline is consistent in its chiastic reflexivity and progression (Blomberg's criterion nine).

The Story of Ruth

One of the longest examples of chiastic development is found in the book of Ruth.[38] Here the story extends itself through several shifts

---

[35] For extensive documentation, see Wenham, *Genesis*, 156–158.

[36] Cf. George W. Coats, *Genesis with an Introduction to Narrative Literature* (Grand Rapids: Eerdmans, 1983), 73–74.

[37] Cf. Victor Hamilton, *The Book of Genesis: Chapters 1–17*, The New International Commentary on the Old Testament (Grand Rapids: Eerdmans, 1990), 2–11.

in scene as it unfolds the story of a desolate widow named Naomi. The figure of Naomi serves to consolidate a larger picture of the plight of Israel during the time of the Judges (1:1). Elimelech, her husband, uproots the family, leaving behind their inheritance to sojourn elsewhere as aliens in a foreign culture. Experiencing the (implied) judgement of God against her, she attempts to return to the context of covenantal blessedness. The misfortunes of Naomi's family have made full restitution seemingly impossible, however, because, as a woman, she cannot inherit the land of her husband. It has passed on to others. Yet suddenly, in the person of Boaz, a hero is found who will champion her cause. In collaboration with Ruth he acts out the necessary redemptive designs that will restore Naomi's position in her homeland. The substance of the story, then, is a recounting of these salvific acts that lead to a point where Naomi, the embittered loser in life, is once again blessed within her community.

While there are many analyses of this drama, it appears, from the balance of the terms and phrases and the careful crafting of the scenes, that a chiastic ordering is present:

A	Naomi becomes destitute. (1:1–5)
B	Deliberations on the road regarding Ruth's and Naomi's future. (1:6–18)
C	Conversation at home about harvest, want and plenty. (1:19–22)
D	Reaping a good harvest. (2:1–17)
E	Premonitions of salvation. (2:18–23)
F	The announcement of "homecoming." (3:1)
E$_1$	Premonitions of salvation. (3:2–6)
D$_1$	Reaping a good harvest. (3:7–15)
C$_1$	Conversations at home about harvest, want and plenty. (3:16–18)
B$_1$	Deliberations on the road regarding Ruth's and Naomi's future. (4:1–12)
A$_1$	Naomi becomes fulfilled. (4:13–17)

---

[38] Cf. Stephen Bertman, "Symmetrical Design in the Book of Ruth," *Journal of Biblical Literature* 84 (1965): 165–168; Edward F. Campbell, Jr., *Ruth,* (Anchor Bible 7; Garden City, New York: Doubleday, 1975), 15–16.

The genealogy tacked onto the end of the story is not intrinsic to the narrative. Rather, it serves to outline the manner in which this "time" of the Judges, characterized by destitution, finds its transition into the era of the Kings, characterized by fulfilment. The star of the genealogy is David, who will function as a national deliverer for his people in a manner analogous to that in which Boaz acted heroically on Naomi's behalf.

The story is told with amazing care.[39] The length of the introduction (1:1–5, English version) and the conclusion (4:13–17) are identical in the Hebrew text—71 words each. There are four clearly defined interior literary panels (1:6–22; 2:1–23; 3:1–15; 3:16–4:12), each functioning as a single "act" in the drama, and each further structured with two separate but related scenes. Moreover, the dramatic events in one of these scenes in each act takes place in a private place, while the other always occurs in a public arena.[40] Not only that—in the first two acts, the "public" scenes happen first, followed by the private scenes, while exactly the reverse is true for the last two acts. Furthermore, the "support cast" to the main characters is also balanced. Although Naomi's story drives the action, typifying the movement of the nation of Israel during these days, the real determiners of action in the story are Boaz and Ruth. Moreover, each of these latter figures is then paired with a complementary "foil": Boaz is aware of a closer relative who has both the responsibility and the opportunity to take on Naomi's case, yet refuses to do so; similarly, Orpah is Naomi's other daughter-in-law who turns back to the family and traditions of Moab, rather than journey with Naomi into the unknown, as Ruth does. Again, when Naomi enters Bethlehem, her old hometown, she is immediately surrounded by a group of women who speak in chorus. This women's chorus appears again as Naomi's consort in the closing scenes. Similarly, whenever Boaz is in the public arena, he is constantly surrounded by a troupe of male "elders" who serve as witnesses, confirming the deeds taking place.

At the heart of it all, in this reading, is the declaration of 3:1—"Naomi her mother-in-law said to her, 'My daughter, I need to seek some security for you, so that it may be well with you.'" This is the

---

[39] Cf. Campbell, *Ruth*, 10–18.

[40] Act I (1:6–22): scene 1 (1:6–18), scene 2 (1:19–22); Act II (2:1–23): scene 1 (2:1–17), scene 2 (2:18–23); Act III (3:1–15): scene 1 (3:1–5), scene 2 (3:6–15); Act IV (3:16–4:12): scene 1 (3:16–18), scene 2 (4:1–12).

quest of Naomi in the drama of the book: a search for security to bring gain out of a situation of great loss and the uncertainty of chaotic times. But it is also the need of Israel in those very times. Thus, the chiastic center of the narrative serves also as the focus or goal of the tale as a whole, giving religious shape to the rationale behind the action of each of the dramatic personae.

It is evident, from this summary, that there is progression and balance to the tale of Ruth. It also appears that the declaration at the center serves well to highlight the overall meaning of the story. In addition to this narrative development there are other elements of the story that seem to confirm these intended patters of literary design. Note the following:

- As noted earlier, both the introductory literary panel (1:1–5) and that which serves as a conclusion (4:13–17) contain exactly 71 words in the Hebrew text. But this clear balance in the economy of telling the story goes much further. The literary panel of Act I (1:6–22) contains 253 words in the Hebrew text; its mirror literary panel, Act IV (3:16–4:12) is composed of 263 Hebrew words. The inner literary panels, Act II (2:1–23) and Act III (3:1–15) are less equally balanced in terms of words used (368/204), probably due, in part, to the differences in location and circumstances. The "public" scene in Act II (2:1–17) takes place during the daytime, when Boaz and Ruth are surrounded by the chorus of workers who participate in the dialogue. The "public" scene in Act III (3:7–15), however, is a nocturnal affair, and does not involve other dramatic personnel beyond Ruth and Boaz.

- There is a clear repetition of Hebrew words in parallel literary panels. In the introduction, for example, Naomi loses her sons (יְלָדֶיהָ) (1:5); in the conclusion she gains a son (אֶת־הַיֶּלֶד) (4:17). In the first Act, Naomi is "empty" (1:21), and in the fourth she will no longer be so (3:17). In Act II Boaz is identified as a "kinsman" (2:1), an appellation that is repeated in the following act (3:2). Similarly, in the second act Boaz remarks that Ruth has taken refuge under the wings (כְּנָפָיו) of refuge of the God of Israel (2:12); in the next (and parallel) act, it is Ruth who declares that she desires to take refuge under Boaz' "wings" (כְנָפֶךָ) (3:9). Again, Boaz is introduced in Act II as a worthy person (אִישׁ גִּבּוֹר חַיִל) (2:1),

a title given then by Boaz to Ruth in the paralleling of Act III
(אֵשֶׁת חַיִל) (3:11). Other examples abound.[41]

- Beyond the paralleling of Hebrew words and phrases
between chiastically mirrored literary panels in the narrative
there is also a reflexive interaction of themes. The flip-flop of
the scenes in each act and its chiastic partner is just one
indication of that. Act I begins with a scene in a public place
(on the road; 1:6–18) and ends in the private scene of Naomi
at home (1:19–22); in a mirror–like reversal, Act IV begins
with the private scene (3:16–18), again in Naomi's home, and
concludes in a public place (in the gate of the city which is,
interestingly, on the road); 4:1–12). Similarly, the first scene
in Act II happens in the public arena of the harvest fields
(2:1–17), while its concluding scene is back in the privacy of
Naomi's home (2:18–23); Act III deals the scenes in
reverse—beginning in Naomi's home (3:1–6), it moves to
culmination back in the harvest fields (3:7–15).

- The continued parallels between the inner acts are striking. In
each Ruth exposes herself at personal risk (from the other
harvesters in Act II; from Boaz in Act III); in each Boaz
invites Ruth to remain under his protection, and pronounces a
blessing upon her; in each Boaz gives food to Ruth. Again,
these examples could be multiplied.

- Even the introduction and the conclusion to the tale have
striking parallels. The names of Mahlon and Chilion,
Naomi's first sons, appear only in these extreme literary
panels. More than that, the order of their names is
reversed in the conclusion (4:9) from that given in the
introduction (1:2).

Obviously some creative hand has worked carefully to arrange
the smaller details of the story in such a way that there appears to be a
larger chiasm that envelops the entire narrative. Given the tendency
toward expressing a large number of details within several of the
literary panels of the story in a chiastically reflexive manner, it seems
as if the inclination toward chiastic story-telling, as a naïve art, may
have been a pervasive thought-process for this author, one which

---

[41] Cf. Campbell, *Ruth*, 13–17.

became operative when bringing together the multiple panels of the tale as a whole.

When Blomberg's criteria for assessing macro-chiasm are applied to this suggested development of the book of Ruth, there is confirmation on all nine points:

1. Many scholars have suggested outlines of the story; none has found universal acceptance.[42]

2. As outlined and described, there are clear examples of parallelism that are widely recognized by scholars.

3. There are both grammatical and conceptual parallels between the reflexively paired sections of the book.

4. Repetition of catchwords and specific phrases highlights the parallelism of the various sections.

5. The introduction and conclusion of the book of Ruth use both verbal and conceptual parallels not found elsewhere throughout the rest of the chiasm.[43]

6. The literary development is compound and complex, supporting chiastic movement over the length of the book.

7. The outline noted here makes use of virtually universally recognized breaks in the text, as suggested also by the chapter developments that have been inserted in the text in recent centuries.

8. In Naomi's words at the center of the chiasm (3:1) is summarized the plight of desolation experienced by Naomi and Ruth, as well as the necessary outcome required and produced by the movements of the story.

9. The outline is consistent and progressive, with no ruptures to detract it from clear chiastic development.

Summary

There are many other examples of chiasm throughout the Hebrew Bible and New Testament that could be cited.[44] A number of

---

[42] Cf. Jacob M. Myers, *The Linguistic and Literary Form of the Book of Ruth* (Leiden: E. J. Brill, 1955), 32.

[43] E.g., the names of Naomi's husband and sons (these latter names in reversed order in the conclusion).

scholars have found macro-chiastic design in various passages of
Hebrew poetry. Bliese, for example, argues that the short prophecy of
Obadiah is made up of six poems set together in $ABC:C_1B_1A_1$
thematic inversion.[45]

Similarly, Lee suggests that the prophecy of Joel, although
somewhat longer than Obadiah, but also largely constructed in verse, is
developed in chiastic fashion around the centering element of 2:10–
32.[46] In this pivotal segment, according to Lee, the focal point of the
message is highlighted: in spite of, and in the context of their weakness
and waywardness, Yahweh still acts on behalf of his people.[47]

In New Testament scholarship there are, besides those already
noted, the many examples of chiasm suggested by Lund,[48] Davids'

---

[44] E.g. Psalm 25 (Cf. H. Möller, "Strophenbau der Psalmen," *Zeitschrift für
die alttestamentliche Wissenschaft 50* [1932]: 240–256; L. Ruppert, "Psalm 25 und
die Grenze Kultorientierter Psalmenexegese," *Zeitschrift für die alttestamentliche
Wissenschaft 84* [1972]: 576–582); Isaiah 5:1–7 (Cf. J. Alec Motyer, *The Prophecy
of Isaiah* [Downers Grove, Illinois: InterVarsity Press, 1993], 68; K. R. Wolfe,
"The Chiastic Structure of Luke-Acts and Some Implications for Worship,"
Southwestern Journal of Theology 22 [1980]: 60–71).

[45] Loren F. Bliese, "Chiastic and Homogeneous Metrical Structures
Enhanced by Word Patterns in Obadiah," *Journal of Translation and Text
Linguistics* 6 (1993): 210–227.

[46] Lena Lee, "The Structure of the Book of Joel," *Kerux* 7 (1993): 4–24.

[47] Joyce Baldwin (*Haggai, Zechariah, Malachi* [Tyndale Old Testament
Commentaries; Downers Grove: InterVarsity Press, 1972]), building on the work of
Lamarche (*Zacharie IX–XIV, Structure Litteraire et Messianisme* [Gabalda, Paris,
1961]), explores an extended, and somewhat complicated, chiastic development of
Zechariah 9–14, 74–81. Although her effort has small merit, particularly with the
sub-units of the passage as a whole, the full sweep of her supposed chiasm does not
adhere to Blomberg's ninth criterion against identifying a chiastic development
with a number of elements shifted out of direct reflexive parallelism.

[48] E.g., among others, I Corinthians 12–14 (Lund, *Chiasmus*, 175–176)
which has a general reflexive development, but which in Lund's treatment, does
not conform well to Blomberg's seventh criterion requiring the breaks between
sub-units of the chiasm to fall in natural places. Also, the prologue to the Fourth
Gospel (Lund, "The Influence of Chiasmus upon the Structure of the Gospels,"
Anglican Theological Review 13 (1931): 42–46), which has been further analysed
by R. Alan Culpepper, "The Pivot of John's Prologue," *New Testament Studies,
27* (1981): 1–31, and Jeff Staley, "The Structure of John's Prologue: Its
Implications for the Gospel's Narrative Structure," *Catholic Biblical Quarterly
48* (1986): 241–264.

understanding of the movements within the letter of James,[49] and Blomberg's analysis of the first seven chapters of 2 Corinthians.[50] Many of these would stand the test of Blomberg's criteria for macro-chiasm on a number of levels.

It is thus fair to say that macro-chiasm as well as micro-chiasm is evident at various places throughout the literature of the Hebrew Bible and the New Testament. Further, it appears that Thomson's criteria and method for locating and analyzing chiastic development on the micro-chiastic level are a beneficial refinement of Lund's initial "laws" regarding chiasm. Finally, Blomberg's criteria for the assessment of macro-chiasm have proved beneficial. They should serve well as tools to determine the validity of the thesis explored in the next section that the farewell discourse in John 13–17 can be read chiastically, and when interpreted from that development there is provided a new and important step in the continuing analysis of the passage.

---

[49] Davids, *James*, 22–29. Blomberg, "Structure," 8, says that Davids' approach is "quite plausible," although Davids does not seem to find a chiastic center worthy of highlighting the entire significance of the letter, as Blomberg's criteria #8 would require.

[50] Blomberg, "Structure," 8–15.

PART III

A CHIASTIC READING OF THE JOHANNINE FAREWELL DISCOURSE

CHAPTER 6

READING THE DISCOURSE

Looking for Reflexive Parallelism

As we noted in Chapter Three, Thomson suggested that the first clue to chiasm in a passage is repetition, and the second clue is the presence of a central element of heightened significance that calls attention to the reflexive mirroring of words and themes in the other elements of the passage across the mid-point of the text. In reading the development of John 13–17 as an unfolding narrative "plot," the following movements emerge.[1]

Jesus had announced, in 12:23ff, that his "hour" had come, and that this hour would bring his death. As chapter 13 opens it appears that Jesus is about to explain how this "hour" will affect his disciples (13:1). The process of setting in motion the execution apparatus is announced (13:2), but sidelined temporarily (until verse 18ff). The first major scene portrays Jesus washing the disciples' feet (13:3–17). Because of the dialogue between Peter and Jesus (13:6–10) the impact of the scene appears to be that of the disciples gaining and retaining a spiritual connection with Jesus (13:8—"share [μερος] with me"). This also appears to be the case because, as the conversation continues and Judas is identified as the betrayer (13:18–30), the narrator explains that "Satan entered into [Judas]" (13:27), with the result that Judas separated himself from Jesus and whatever glory there might be

---

[1] Cf. R. Alan Culpepper, *Anatomy of the Fourth Gospel: A Study in Literary Design* (Philadelphia: Fortress, 1983), 77–98. See also the method of reading the biblical text described by Charles H. Talbert in *Reading Luke* (New York: Crossroad, 1989), 1–6, and in *Reading Corinthians* (New York: Crossroad, 1989), xiii.

surrounding Jesus in this special hour, opting instead to go out into the night [νύξ] (13:30).

Now the "hour" apparently begins, and Jesus announces it with a summary statement regarding glorification, his leaving, and the command to love (13:35). These are rolled into one another with such continuity that they appear to be a single great declaration.

There is a brief period of dialogue with Peter (13:36, 13:37), Thomas (14:5), Philip (14:8) and Judas (14:22) interacting with Jesus, raising questions in response to his statements. Peter has previously spoken to Jesus in both the foot-washing episode (13:6–9) and in the conversation in which Judas is identified as betrayer (13:24–25). Peter seems to have a bold and assertive relationship with Jesus that prompts him to react quickly to Jesus' actions and statements. After 13:36, however, the dialogue appears to be more round-table, with different disciples entering the dialogue at various points. Thus it appears, at this point, that the tone of the narrative shifts from action to a more formal expression of conversation and discourse.

Even though Peter asks Jesus where he is going (13:36), the focus turns immediately (and rather unexpected) to Peter's denial of Jesus (13:37–38). The suddenness with which that topic enters the conversation at that particular point stands out. There was nothing in the context to prod Jesus' challenging response to Peter. For some reason the intervening verses (13:37–38) seem to move the dialogue somewhat abruptly in a different direction.

Chapter 14:1–14 unfolds with a fairly consistent movement. Jesus is going away to his Father's house (14:2–3) to take up his residence and prepare residences for the disciples. They will be able to travel the road to the Father's house provided they attach themselves to Jesus (14:6). The unique connection between Jesus and his Father is further explained in 14:8–14, yet Jesus indicates that the disciples are able also to enter into this special relationship (14:11–14).

A new theme develops in 14:15. It is related to the previous section in terms of a call for the connectedness of the disciples with Jesus, and through him with the Father. Yet now the nature of that connectedness is spelled out as a ministry of the παράκλητος ("Advocate") (14:16) who is identified as the "Spirit of truth." It is in this context that the connection between Father, Jesus and disciples is confirmed and nurtured (14:18–24), leading back to a specific identification of the ministry of the "Advocate" again in 14:26. But the Advocate disappears from the scene until 15:26, and Jesus develops these themes no further until then.

Now the tone changes again. Rather than focusing on the relationship between Jesus, the Father and the disciples, nurtured by the Advocate, Jesus speaks about his peace giving the disciples fortitude in the troubling times that will follow his departure. The language of 14:27 mirrors that of 14:1, the first time in the discourse that a specific repetition is apparent. There does not, however, appear to be a broader repetition of ideas or themes at this moment. Jesus instead continues the new theme of the peace that his disciples will receive through this knowledge, even in the context of a troubling situation.

The last phrase of 14:31 is enigmatic. Jesus suddenly says, "Rise, let us be on our way." Yet no movement appears to take place, and chapter 15 marches on into a clearly different, though related, element of discourse. It is apparent that the unifying theme of the first eight verses is Jesus' teaching about the vine and branches. At the heart of his monologue is a call and challenge for the disciples to "abide in me" [μείνατε ἐν ἐμοί] (15:4, 5, 6, 7), repeated in some form at least eight times.

At 15:9 there is a moment of indecisive apprehension for the reader. The Greek term καθώς ("As") sometimes signals the start of a new thought development. Yet there are three more references to "abide in" in 15:9–10, and these appear to wed the ideas of these verses very closely to the theme of 15:1–8. 15:11 seems to finish the thought begun in the previous verses because of the reference to Jesus' joy being in the disciples [ἐν ὑμῖν] which appears to imply again the "abiding in" continuity.

With 15:12 we have a clear reiteration of 13:34. Not only that, but 15:17 repeats the mutual love command once again. The intervening verses pick up the theme of masters and servants first expressed in 13:16 and the exhortation to bear fruit from 15:1–8. They also reflect the commissioning theses of 13:31–33. The dominant theme of 15:12–17 seems to be an intentional repetition of the major ideas of 13:31–33.

As we move into 15:18ff parallels with and repetitions of things stated earlier leap out with great constancy. 15:18–25 picks up the contrast between the power and attitude of the "world" [ὁ κόσμος] that appears prominent in 14:27–31. Similarly 15:26–27 appear to be a reiteration of the words and ideas 14:25–26. Suddenly it seems as if

we are backing our way along the course recently travelled. 16:1–4a
continue the themes of 15:26–27, giving substance to them in the
specific situation of excommunication from synagogues. 16:4a ties
15:26–16:4a together as a package, and again brings thoughts of
repetition from 15:25.

Jesus' statement in 16:5 that "none of you asks me, 'Where are
you going?'" reminds us immediately of Peter's question to that effect
back in 13:36. Yet the theme of 16:4b–15 is largely parallel to that of
14:15–24 where Jesus promises to send the παράκλητος
("Advocate") who strengthens those who know Jesus and the Father,
but works in opposition to whatever belongs to "the world."

16:16–28 brings back Jesus' talk of leaving "in a little while"
and the comfort to be provided by the Father that was first presented in
14:1–14. In fact, just as at the center of the earlier passage Thomas
and Philip bring questions about the meaning of Jesus' words, so also
at the center of this section the disciples as a group are given to
questioning. The section ends similarly to the manner in which 14:1
began, with straightforward declaration by Jesus that he is returning to
the Father.

Then, when it seems as if clarity in all things has arrived (16:29)
and the disciples are affirming confidence in the teachings Jesus has
spoken, the dark shadows of 13:36–38 return. Just as there Jesus
declared solidarity with the disciples in the trauma of the times ahead
and Jesus returned a prophecy of denial, so here in 16:29–33, after the
disciples together speak declarations of great faith, Jesus foretells their
communal desertion from him.

As chapter 17 opens Jesus takes command of the group in a way
that is reminiscent of the beginning of chapter 13. Not only that, but
Jesus repeats the line from 13:1 which declares that "the hour has
come" (17:1). In 13:3 the evangelist tells us that Jesus knew "that the
Father had given all things into his hands." In 17:2 Jesus declares, in
his prayer, that the Father "has given him authority over all people."
Then, in parallel to the footwashing episode in chapter 13, Jesus now
announces, in chapter 17, that he has prepared the disciples to belong
to the Father. Further, he declares that all of them have, in fact,
become one with the Father and Jesus "except the one destined to be
lost" (17:12). This is located, in the flow of the prayer, in a position
virtually identical to Jesus' declaration during the footwashing
ceremony that "not all of you are clean" (13:11).

As Jesus concludes his prayer in 17:21–24 he makes reference to the shared glory of the Father and himself, repeating again the theme (and almost the wording) of 13:31–33. The culmination of the prayer is a definitive declaration that shared love will become the norm (17:25–26). These words repeat, in fulfilled form, the injunction of the new commandment stated in 15:12–17 and earlier in 13:34–35.

Weighing the Evidence

From this reading of the farewell discourse the first stage of Thomson's investigation is met. There is, indeed, repetition of terms and ideas that balance themselves in somewhat equivalent measure on either side of a pivotal center. In broad outline, the following repetitious elements are most noticeable in John 13–17:

- Jesus is about to leave the disciples and go to the Father (13:1, 3, 33, 36; 14:2–4, 12, 28–29; 16:5–7, 16, 28).
- Jesus will be betrayed by Judas (13:2, 11, 18, 21–30), disowned by Peter (13:38), and deserted by the Eleven (16:32).
- The disciples are chosen by Jesus (13:18; 15:19).
- Jesus issues the "new commandment" to love each other (13:34–35; 15:12–17).
- "Asking" and "receiving" are encouraged (14:13–14; 16:23–24, 26).
- "Obedience" to Jesus' "commands" is the sign of "love" for him (14:15, 21, 23–24; 15:9–10).
- Jesus promises the coming of the παράκλητος ("Advocate") to "testify" in and through the disciples (14:16–18, 26; 15:26–27; 16:7–11, 12–15).
- Jesus declares his "peace" upon the disciples (14:1, 27; 16:33).
- Jesus promises "joy" (15:11; 16:20–22).
- Jesus foretells the "hatred" of the world (15:18–25; 16:1–4).

Clearly there is sufficient repetition of words and ideas in the Johannine farewell discourse to suggest the possibility of chiastic reflexivity. Virtually all who read John 13–17 take note of these obvious repetitions.[2]

The second stage of chiastic investigation, according to Thomson, calls for a closer look at the correspondence between parallel repetitive sections, and the manner in which the movement of thought in the elements relates to the conceptual development of the whole. Based on the movement of plot in the discourse, an initial broad understanding of the reflexive movement would look something like this:

A   Symbolic Union with Jesus (13:1–35)—an act of
        sanctification (footwashing)
B   Themes of Leaving, Denial, Trouble and Comfort
                (13:36–14:31)
C   Life Connections (15:1–17)
B_1 Themes of Trouble, Comfort, Leaving and Denial
                (15:18–16:33)
A_1 Symbolic Union with Jesus (17:1–26)—an act of
        sanctification (prayer)

Indeed, those who look for elements of parallelism that may be read chiastically in the Johannine farewell discourse begin here.[3] Yet while the simplicity and thematic clarity of the above chiastic reading has inherent integrity, it is too brief to deal with the larger complexity of the two major discourse sections, 13:35–14:31 and 15:18–16:33.

It would be helpful to find further lines of repetition, parallelism and inversion within these sections in order to give fuller shape to the chiastic reading. Indeed, it would be most helpful, at this point, to use each of Blomberg's criterion for assessing macro-chiasm, and measure the extent to which these initial perceptions of chiasm might be shown to have fuller substance. To this we next turn.

---

[2] Cf. Brown, *Gospel*, 588–594.
[3] Cf. Francis J. Moloney, *The Gospel of John* (Collegeville, Minnesota: The Liturgical Press, 1998), 24.

CHAPTER 7

TESTING THE READING

Criteria for Macro-Chiasm

As noted in Chapter Three, Blomberg's refinement of the criteria by which instances of perceived macro-chiasm are assessed has provided a measuring tool that gives significant objectivity to what has often become a very subjective field of investigation. All of Blomberg's nine criteria are useful in our reading of the Johannine farewell discourse, although criterion 2, 3, and 7 are most essential in determining the strength of chiastic movement in John 13–17. In this chapter all nine of the criteria will be used to test the hypothesis, with a particular emphasis on those that are of most significance in confirming or disproving it.

CRITERION #1: OTHER APPROACHES TO LITERARY DEVELOPMENT MUST PROVE PROBLEMATIC

Blomberg's first criterion is easily met when looking for an alternative structure to those most often offered in reading John 13–17. There are, indeed, many problems in perceiving the overall structure of the Johannine farewell discourse. The logic of the conversations between Jesus and the disciples seems to break down, at times, if it is read as taking place during a single meal and happening in continuous sequence.[1] There is repetition of words and phrases and themes that appear to take place in very short order, but which also seem to happen

---

[1] E.g., Peter's question of Jesus' departure destination in 13:36 seemingly ignored by Jesus in 16:5; the mystifying call to leave at 14:31 that seems not to be acted upon.

in isolation from one another.[2] Furthermore, the transitions between
14:31 and 15:1, as well as that between the first part of 16:4 and the
conclusion of that verse, are quite abrupt, and seem to thwart simple
literary organizational solutions.

A number of general solutions to the difficulties presented by
these unusual features of the text have been offered. Current research
on the Fourth Gospel can be summarized, in fact, in three large areas of
investigation: literary criticism, historical criticism and theological
criticism.[3]   While some literary critics focus on the history of
composition,[4] many have developed theories that analyse the gospel as
holding together with integrity in its current form.[5] Historical critics
have attempted to recover the history and successive forms of the
gospel,[6] and theological studies have traced themes that appear
throughout the gospel.[7]

---

[2] E.g., the statements regarding the Advocate in 14:15–26 and those in
15:26–16:15.

[3] These are the general distinctions made by Robert Kysar in "The Fourth
Gospel. A Report on Recent Research," *Aufstieg und Niedergang der römischen
Welt* 25 (1985): 2506–2568. See also D. F. Tolmie, *Jesus' Farewell to the
Disciples: John 13:1–17:26 in Narratological Perspective* (Leiden,: E. J. Brill,
1995), 1–7.

[4] E.g., Robert Thomson Fortna, *The Fourth Gospel and its Predecessors:
From Narrative Source to Present Gospel* (Philadelphia: Fortress, 1988); Barnabas
Lindars, *Behind the Fourth Gospel* (London, SPCK, 1971); James Louis Martyn,
History and Theology in the Fourth Gospel (Nashville: Abingdon, 1979).

[5] E.g., Culpepper, *Anatomy*; Mlakuzhyil, *Christocentric*; Jeff Staley, *The
Print's First Kiss: A Rhetorical Investigation of the Implied Reader in the Fourth
Gospel* (Atlanta: Scholars Press, 1988).

[6] E.g., Raymond E. Brown, *The Community of the Beloved Disciple: The
Life, Loves and Hates of an Individual Church in New Testament Times* (New
York: Paulist, 1979); J. Wagner, *Auferstehung und Leben. Joh 11,1–12, 19 als
Spiegel johanneischer Redaktions- und Theologiegeschichte* (Regensburg:
Pustet, 1988).

[7] E.g., the identity of Jesus—Herman Ridderbos, *The Gospel of John: A
Theological Commentary* (Grand Rapids: Eerdmans, 1997); the nature of the
Paraclete—John Painter, "The Influence of Christian Prophecy on the Johannine
Portrayal of the Paraclete and Jesus," *New Testament Studies* 25 (1978): 113–123;
D. A. Carson, "The Function of the Paraclete in John 16:7–11," *Journal of Biblical
Literature* 98 (1979): 547–566; the identity of the Beloved Disciple—M. Pamment,
"The Fourth Gospel's Beloved Disciple," *Expository Times* 94 (1983): 363–367;
the meaning of the footwashing scene—H. Weiss, "Footwashing in the Johannine
Community," *Novum Testamentum* 21 (1979): 298–325; A. J. Hultgren, "The
Johannine Footwashing (13:1–11): A Symbol of Eschatological Hospitality," *New
Testament Studies* 28 (1982): 539–546; J. C. Thomas, *Footwashing in John 13 and
the Johannine Community* (Sheffield: JSOT, 1991).

Moreover, recent studies have approached John 13–17 looking for comparisons with other similar types of "farewell discourse" in hopes of finding alternative models for understanding the development of these chapters.[8] As the Fourth Gospel positions this material, Jesus has finished his ministry, and the "hour" of glory and death has arrived.[9] But before that hour takes its bloody toll, the main characters of the story pause to reflect. What is the significance of all that Jesus has done? Is there still, among the disciples, a lingering insecurity about his identity? How will the events that are building to crisis level affect them? Where will they find strength and security when they leave the safety of this intimate setting?

It is these matters that Jesus addresses in his lengthy table talk. The discourse itself begs to be treated as a coherent literary unit.[10] Narrative signals (13:2; 18:1) indicate that all of the action, dialogue and monologue take place within a single location (a guest room where Jesus and the disciples are sharing an evening meal) and at a single temporal occasion in the gospel's narrative sequence (on the night before Jesus' crucifixion). The mealtime activities which open chapter 13 become the opportunity for Jesus to engage his disciples in conversations about their identity, as well as begin to explain the next stage in the process of "glorification" that is just ahead. These discussions continue with recurring exploration of the same themes through the end of chapter 16. After that point Jesus offers a prayer in which he raises, in summary form, many of the same issues of identity and future expectations as were expressed in the preceding verses. Now, however, there seems to be added a new dimension in which the element of "fulfillment"[11] introduced in 13:1 is amplified and given more concrete shape.

---

[8] Cf. Fernando F. Segovia, *The Farewell of the Word* (Minneapolis: Augsburg Fortress, 1991), who sets this discourse in the context of other "farewell discourses" in the literature of Hellenic and pre-Hellenic times.

[9] John 12:20–13:1.

[10] Cf. Thomas Brodie, *The Gospel According to John: A Literary and Theological Commentary* (New York: Oxford University Press, 1993), 427–446; Brown, *Gospel*, 559–562; Segovia, *Farewell*, 1–58.

[11] ...εἰδὼς ὁ Ἰησοῦς ὅτι ἦλθεν αὐτοῦ ἡ ὥρα ἵνα μεταβῇ ἐκ τοῦ κόσμου τούτου πρὸς τὸν πατέρα, ἀγαπήσας τοὺς ἰδίους τοὺς ἐν τῷ κόσμῳ εἰς τέλος ἠγάπησεν αὐτούς. ("Now before the festival of the Passover, Jesus knew that his hour had come to depart from this world and go to the Father. Having loved his own who were in the world, he loved them to the end.")

While historical and textual criticism have illuminated both the multi-layered character of the community in which the gospel had its beginnings [12] and the manner in which it appears now to be stratified,[13] literary analysis[14] has helped to recover a sense of plot and dramatic development of theme.[15] Within the gospel as a whole, these chapters form a unique interlude,[16] creating an interpretive bridge between the public ministry of Jesus and the hour of his glory that looms as both a threat and a promise. White calls it "John's introduction to the story of Christ's passion."[17] Schnackenburg suggested that Jesus' "Abschieds-worte" offer a message of consolation ("Trost") that continues to be of significance for all who wait in the hope of the redeemer's ("Erlöser") return.[18]

Recent scholarship has reaffirmed the integrity of the Johannine farewell discourse as a literary unit,[19] and has explored further issues

---

[12] See Martyn, *History*; John Painter, *The Quest for the Messiah*, 2d ed. (Nashville: Abingdon, 1993), 33–135.

[13] For a detailed examination of the written and oral sources circulating in the first century, along with a careful hypothesis regarding stages of development in the present textual form of the gospel, see Brown, *Gospel*, xxxiv–xxxix; Painter, *Quest*, 61–118.

[14] See Gail R. O'Day, "Toward a Narrative-Critical Study of John," *Interpretation* 49 (1995): 341–346.

[15] Cf. R. Alan Culpepper, "The Plot of John's Story of Jesus," *Interpretation* 49 (1995): 347–358.

[16] Cf. George R. Beasley-Murray, *John* (Word Biblical Commentary 36; Waco, Texas: Word, 1987) 222–227.

[17] R. E. O. White, *The Night He Was Betrayed* (Grand Rapids: Eerdmans, 1982), 10.

[18] Rudolf Schnackenburg, *Ihr werdet mich sehen: Die Abschiedsworte Jesu nach Joh 13–17* (Freiburg/Basel/Vienna: Herder, 1985). Schnackenburg's reflections were written originally as a series of 24 meditations published during Advent and Lent.

[19] Cf. C. K. Barrett, *The Gospel according to St John* (London: SPCK, 1978), 436; Beasley-Murray, *John*, xci–xcii; Joseph Blank, *The Gospel according to St. John*, Vol. 2 (New York: Crossroad, 1981), 11–15; Brodie, *Gospel*, 427–440; Brown, *Gospel*, 545–547; Brevard Childs, *The New Testament as Canon: An Introduction* (Philadelphia: Fortress, 1984), 136–142; Culpepper, *Anatomy*, 94–95; David Deeks, "The Structure of the Fourth Gospel," *New Testament Studies 15* (1968–69): 110–119; Gerard Sloyan, *John* (Atlanta: John Knox, 1988), ix; Mark W. G. Stibbe, *John's Gospel* (New York: Routledge, 1994), 11, 25–27; Segovia, *Farewell*; E. C. Webster, "Pattern in the Fourth Gospel," 230–257 in D. J. A. Clines, D. M. Gunn, and A. J. Hauser (editors), *Art and Meaning: Rhetoric in Biblical Literature* (JSOT Supplement Series 19; Sheffield: JOST, 1982), 231, 249–250.

of genre.[20] There are some scholars, like Blank,[21] who believe that it is possible to identify a unique genre of biblical literature of a type which he titles "farewell discourses." He and others see representations of this genre in the Hebrew Bible stories of Jacob pronouncing blessings on his sons before his death,[22] Joshua taking final leave of the Israelites at the close of his life,[23] and the purported "last words" of David.[24] As each of these figures approached the end of life or the close of a particular segment of his leadership career, he made a public address that served to summarise elements of his theological perspectives, and sometimes the larger worldview through which he perceived comprehensive structure in the universe. In this context, according to Blank, the great one would establish criteria by which the community that remained after his passing would shape its existence.

Lussier[25] agrees with Blank that it is possible to document this particular biblical literary genre, and finds similar New Testament

---

[20] In an illuminating review article of five recent studies of the Farewell Discourse ("Der Weggang Jesu: Neue Arbeiten zu Joh 13–17," *Biblische Zeitschrift* 40 [1996]: 236–250), Hans-Josef Klauck, summarises the major approaches to these chapters in the following manner: genre investigations ("Gattungsfrage") as typified by Martin Winter (*Das Vermächtnis Jesus und die Abschiedsworte der Vater: Gattungsgeschichtliche Untersuchung der Vermächtnisrede im Blick auf Joh 13–17* [Forschungen zur Religion und Literatur des Alten und Neuen Testaments 161; Göttingen: Vandenhoeck & Ruprecht, 1994]); narrative analysis ("Erzähltextanalyse") as presented by D. F. Tolmie (*Jesus' Farewell to the Disciples: John 13:1–17:26 in Narratological Perspective* [Leiden: E. J. Brill, 1995]); reader-response ("Textlinguistik") approaches as summarised by J. Neugebauer (*Die eschatologischen Aussagen in den johanneischen Abschiedsreden: Eine Untersuchung zu Johannes 13–17* [Stuttgart: W. Kohlhammer, 1995]); historical development theory as brought to light by A. Dettwiler (*Die Gegenwart des Erhöhten: Eine exegetische Studie zu den johanneischen Abschiedsreden [Joh 13,31–16,33]* unter besonderer Berücksichtigung ihres Relecture-Charakters [Göttingen: Vandenhoeck & Ruprecht, 1995]); and early Christian theological reflection ("Nachösterliche Hermeneutik") as understood by C. Hoegen-Rohls (*Der nachösterliche Johannes: Die Abschiedsreden als hermeneutischer Schlüssel zum vierten Evangelium* [Tübingen: J. C. B. Mohr, 1996]).

[21] Blank, *Gospel*, 13.

[22] Genesis 49. See also E. Cortès, *Los discursos de adiós de Gn 49 a Jn 13– 17: Pistas para la historia de un género literario en la antigua literatura judía. Colectanea San Paciano 23* (Barcelona: Herder, 1976).

[23] Joshua 22–24.

[24] 1 Chronicles 28–29.

[25] Earnest Lussier, *Christ's Farewell Discourse* (New York: Alba House, 1979), 3–4.

examples in Paul's speech to the Ephesian elders when he believes he
will not see them again,[26] the Pauline farewell to Timothy,[27] the
Petrine "testament,"[28] and the apocalyptic address of Jesus in Mark
13. In this view there is some degree of commonality in the biblical
recitations of the speeches given by leaders at the close of their time
with individuals and communities formed or shaped in significant
ways under their care.

Winter widens the survey of related materials more broadly,
focusing on other elements of the Jewish literary tradition. Beginning
with Isaac's blessing on his twin sons,[29] Jacob's parting beatific vision
for his family,[30] and Moses' final testament to Israel in the book of
Deuteronomy,[31] Winter then moves on to elements of both the
Apocrypha[32] and the Pseudepigrapha,[33] including a cursory glance at
Pseudo-Philo's *Biblical Antiquities*. Winter concludes that the farewell
discourse in the Fourth Gospel was deliberately modelled by the
Johannine school on such writings as an attempt to create Jesus' own
testament for his disciples at the close of his life.[34]

While there is value in comparing these departure scenes, with
their exhortations, it is difficult to find a true literary connection
between them. Each address is different in form and style, and none is
set within a larger literary framework that would call to mind one of
the earlier speeches. Similarly, there is no clear link between any of
them and the substance of the Johannine farewell discourse; there does
not appear to be either a common literary tradition connecting the
stories[35] or a definitive structure giving clear and similar literary
development to the greatly divergent moods and expressions found
among these several different stories. Jacob's death litany (Genesis

---

[26] Acts 20:17–38.

[27] II Timothy 3:1–4:8.

[28] II Peter.

[29] Genesis 27:1–40.

[30] Genesis 47–50.

[31] Winter focuses especially on chapters 31–34.

[32] Tobit's words of advise to his son Tobias when he suspects that he
(Tobit) is about to be killed (4:1–21), and those he delivers in old age to Tobias as a
death-bed last will and testament (14:1–11); Matthias final testament and
instructions to his sons at death (1 Maccabees 2:49–70).

[33] 1 Enoch, 2 Enoch and Jubilees.

[34] Winter, *Das Vermächtnis Jesu*, 288–289.

[35] Each of the examples cited is located in a different text and tradition of
scripture, and none are linked by way of common authorship.

49:1–28), for example, is a prophetic projection, combining elements of the temperament of each son with political moments from the future history of their tribal descendants. Joshua's final speech (Joshua 23–24) contains elements of the typical Suzerain-Vassal covenant in brief form, as a renewal moment for Israel. David gets three "dying moments," each unlike the others. His "last words," as recorded in II Samuel 23:1–7, are a typical "psalm" with no references either to his own death or to future generations. David's first parting words with Solomon (I Kings 2:1–9) are stern and vindictive, while his other deathbed address is a combination of words to the officials of his kingdom, including Solomon (I Chronicles 28:2–10; 20–21), to the nation as a whole in assembly (I Chronicles 29:1–5), and to God in the form of a psalm and a prayer (I Chronicles 29:10–19). The New Testament examples are even more diverse in character and literary positioning: Paul's final address to the Ephesian elders at Miletus (Acts 20:17–38); the death notice at the conclusion of 2 Timothy (4:6–8); the urgings of an aging leader (2 Peter 1:12–15); and the apocalyptic exhortation of Jesus (Revelation 22:12–20).

A much better case might be made for what many believe is the clearest biblical parallel to the Johannine farewell discourse: the book of Deuteronomy. When viewed as a whole, Deuteronomy reads as a kind of last will and testament for Moses. In it he reviews the years of Israel's journey since leaving Egypt. He also attempts to vindicate his role of leadership with the people. Further, he gives parting instructions that he intends to bring them into the next phase of their existence, just beyond the river where they are camped.

The parallels with the Johannine farewell discourse are obvious: a leader facing death, a journey of faith for a new community, a transition into a new phase of existence for those left behind. Because of that, Blank, in fact, is willing to assert "that John... took the form consciously from Deuteronomy."[36] He cites two literary clues to support his conjecture: first, he finds the concluding prayer of Jesus in John 17 strikingly parallel to Moses' concluding song and blessing in Deuteronomy 32–33; second, "as in Deuteronomy, the literary genre is pressed into the service of a new message that is linked with the older Jesus-tradition."[37] In Blank's assessment, biblical texts that conform to his identification of a genre of "farewell discourse" heighten the authority of these "final" words spoken, since they are like a will or

---

[36] Blank, *Gospel*, 13.
[37] Ibid.

testament handed over to the community of faith by its irreplaceable founder at the moment of death or departure. Further, just as the authentic farewell speech of a great leader carries unusual weight of authority, so also among those writings that might appear after the leader's death, any which can claim to arise in the moment of exit would receive special weight and importance.

Blank is likely overstating the case in his attempt to develop a unique biblical literary genre of "farewell discourse," particularly in view of the lack of cohesion between the examples he cites. There is reason to suspect, however, that these instances of famous last words in Christian scripture may be imitations of a genre among the writings of the ancient Mediterranean world. As Beasley-Murray notes,[38] the literary genre of "farewell discourse" or "testament" is widely known in both early Judaism and the larger Hellenistic world.[39] In fact, according to Stauffer,[40] the farewell discourse form reached its most developed configuration in Jewish literature. Indeed, there appear to be at least two basic expressions of the Jewish model of farewell discourse. First, there is a primary type showing scenes which portray a figure who stands as mediator between God and humans delivering a revelatory address upon which future generations ought to base their values and activities.[41] Secondly, there is a less common form, in which a direct epiphany of God or angels to a prominent religious figure is described. These latter types of farewell discourse are most often couched in language that attempts to convey the sense of either a waking or dreaming journey into heaven.

The tradition of farewell discourse appears to have an even earlier origin in the literature of antiquity.[42] According to Segovia,[43] there were at least three different kinds of "farewell speeches" among Greco-Roman writings. Some were the oracles of famous men who had come to the end of their lives; others were the speeches of those anticipating their imminent transfiguration and ascent to a higher plain

---

[38] Beasley-Murray, *John*, 222–223.

[39] Cf. Winter, *Das Vermächtnis Jesu.*

[40] E. Stauffer, "Abschiedsreden," *Reallexikon für Antike und Christentum 1* (1950): 29–35 as cited in Segovia, *Farewell*, 5–6.

[41] E.g., *The Testament of Job, The Testaments of the Twelve Patriarchs, The Testament of Moses.* See James Charlesworth, editor, *The Old Testament Pseudepigrapha*, Vol. 1 (Garden City, New York: Doubleday, 1983), 773–995.

[42] Cf. William S. Kurz, "Luke 22:14–38 and Greco-Roman and Biblical Farewell Addresses," *Journal of Biblical Literature* 104 (1985): 251–268.

[43] Segovia, *Farewell*, 6–7.

of existence; and a third group involved the addresses of gods who appeared in human disguise prior to their return from a time of meandering with mortals.

There are two major forms of comparison that are drawn between the Johannine farewell discourse and this complex miscellany of similar speeches found in the literary genres of its times.[44] On the one hand, some have found formal elements of similarity between both the context and the content of John 13–17 and these antecedent examples.[45] The point of this comparison seems to indicate that a farewell discourse, such as the one found in John 13–17, is used to form a bridge between the life and teachings of Jesus (John 2–12) and the passion narrative that follows (John 18–20). On the other hand, some, like Segovia, have used literary comparisons of the Johannine farewell discourse both to define the formulation of the elements of the discourse[46] and also to show how similar elements of the discourse are bound together in complementary literature. Segovia has investigated these comparisons at length,[47] and believes that there is ample warrant for linking John 13–17 to these other examples of the farewell genre.[48] He states the matter in this way:

> The present text of the farewell speech undoubtedly did represent to someone, somewhere, at some time, not only a unified and coherent literary whole, but also a proper and meaningful form of communication with an audience—an artistic and strategic whole. This is a fundamental aspect of the farewell that the redactional resolution has largely disregarded.[49]

---

[44] Cf. Howard-Brook, *Becoming Children*, 290–292.

[45] Besides Cortez, *Los discursos*, and Stauffer, "Abschiedsreden," see also Johannes Munck, "Discours d'adieu dans le Nouveau Testament et dans la littérature biblique," in *Aux sources de la tradition chrétienne: Mélanges offerts à M. Maurice Goguel*, 155–170 (Bibliothèque théologique. Neuchâtel and Paris: Delachaux & Niestlé, 1950), and William S. Kurz, "Luke 22:14–38 and Greco-Roman and Biblical Farewell Addresses," *Journal of Biblical Literature* 104 (1985): 251–68.

[46] Cf. Segovia, *Farewell*, 7–13.

[47] Ibid., 4–20, 308–319.

[48] Ibid., 319.

[49] Ibid., 48. Cf. also Brodie, *Gospel*, 427: "Such discourses, therefore, had a dramatic unity, and the fact that John 13–17, with the meal, farewell, and prayer, follows that convention, provides additional evidence of these chapters' unity."

Still, Segovia's vagueness about the direct correspondence between the Johannine farewell discourse and other examples of similar literature is indicative of the study at this time: to date no one has given satisfactory definition of either a clear farewell discourse form nor a literary dependence between any of the several expressions cited above.[50] Simoens has explored the relationship between John 13–17 and the farewell of Moses in the book of Deuteronomy at length; yet, as we shall see below, his connections are less than convincing. At this point in the research questions of genre do not seem to provide helpful insights for determining the form or comprehensive integrity of John 13–17.

Nevertheless, the difficulties of literary development in the Johannine farewell discourse remain. The most obvious of these problems is found in Jesus' command in 14:31— Ἐγείρεσθε, ἄγωμεν ἐντεῦθεν.[51]

This command seems strange in its present location[52] since apparently none among his little troupe responds at that moment by making efforts to vacate the room. In fact, as the discourse continues to unfold, Jesus himself appears to continue his speech without making any further references to departure until the opening verse of chapter 18. Sloyan amusingly suggests that a copyist added these words because he was tired from his tedious efforts at reproducing this lengthy discourse, and wanted to get up and walk about a bit.[53] There are at least five more serious approaches to resolving the difficulties posed by this unusual interruption in the literary flow of the discourse.

Delayed Physical Movement

Following Westcott's lead,[54] Morris[55] and Hendriksen[56] suggest that Jesus actually began his departure from the room in the moments

---

[50] See H. Ridderbos, *Gospel*, 481–482.

[51] "Rise, let us be on our way."

[52] Bultmann, *John*, 459.

[53] Sloyan, *John*, 185. There is no manuscript evidence to support such a stretch of the imagination.

[54] B. F. Westcott, *The Gospel According to St. John* (Grand Rapids: Eerdmans, 1954), 187.

following this word of instruction. Since there would be a span of a few minutes during the ensuing shuffle, as the disciples stretched and dressed themselves for the journey, Jesus must have used the time to explain further some of the matters that he had already begun to address. In this perspective all of the material recorded in chapters 15 and 16 is actually the continuation of Jesus' conversations and instructions as the group prepared to leave the room. When all were ready to exit, Jesus led his troupe in the prayer that is now found in chapter 17. Hendriksen, in his explanation of this activity, went so far as to test the amount of time necessary to read chapters 15 and 16. He says that, "speaking calmly and deliberately, without any attempt to rush himself, Jesus may have uttered the contents of chapters 15, 16, and 17 within a period of *ten minutes!*"[57]

Of course, if indeed Jesus and the disciples are in the process of exiting after Jesus' insistent call to leave, there is no need to regard the command of 14:31 as creating any disturbance in the flow of the text. It makes perfect sense where it exists. Nothing needs to be rearranged, nor is there a requirement to posit antecedent sources that might have been edited poorly. The command, as it stands and where it stands, is perfectly suitable, according to this interpretation, and can be read as is without becoming illogical.[58]

Psychological Movement

Most scholars do not believe that Jesus would have continued to speak such powerful words of challenge during the confused scramble to depart. A second theory, taking an entirely different approach,

---

[55] Morris, *John*, 661: "Anyone who has tried to get a group of a dozen or so to leave a particular place at a particular time will appreciate that it usually takes more than one brief exhortation to accomplish this. There is nothing at all unlikely in an interval between the uttering of the words and the departure of the group. And if an interval, then there is no reason why Jesus should not have continued to speak during it."

[56] William Hendriksen, *New Testament Commentary: Exposition of the Gospel According to John* (Grand Rapids: Baker, 1953, 1954), 290.

[57] Hendriksen, *Exposition,* 290.

[58] Interestingly, for all the devotional focus Hendriksen brings to bear on Jesus' interaction with his disciples, he fails to take into account the character of the prayer in chapter 17. It is not the kind of extended petition one tosses off while straightening up the room.

appeared already in the sixteenth century. Calvin suggested an interpretation of this command of Jesus in 14:31 from a perspective of psychological rather than physical movement. According to Calvin, Jesus never meant to tell the disciples to get up and go at this point. Instead of signalling an expedition out from the room, Jesus "intended to exhort the disciples to render the same obedience to God, of which they beheld in him so illustrious an example."[59] The call to "get up and go there" is designed to elevate their thinking to a higher plane. It leads naturally, in Calvin's understanding, into the parable of the vine and branches. As Jesus develops his themes in those verses, immediately following this command to arise and leave, he gives a type of verbal object lesson for his group in which he shows the disciples how to arise and where to go psychologically, volitionally and spiritually.

Among the great exegetes of the twentieth century Dodd has continued to champion this psychological interpretation of Jesus' call in 14:31. "There is no movement in space," he says; "the advance on the enemy is Christ's own resolve to do the Father's will."[60] In other words, Jesus is bucking up his troops to engage in a higher form of spiritual warfare.

More recently, Brodie[61] and Moloney[62] have asserted a similar position. Brodie points to the fact that Jesus had already spoken clearly about his imminent death near the close of chapter 14. It is therefore likely that Jesus has already begun a process of abject self-emptying. The call in 14:31 is a psychological cue that begins the resurrection process for Jesus, and with him, the disciples:

> But precisely by reaching such a low point, by dying, the seed comes to new life. And so when Jesus says, 'Arise, let us go from here,' he is not saying that they must leave the room. He is talking, as he did, for instance, to Nicodemus and the woman of Samaria, on a higher challenging level, the level of spiritual birth and development. He is evoking the whole process of growth which is found first of all in himself, but it includes also those in whom his divine Spirit has been planted (cf. vv 12–24) and in whom it has begun to take root (cf. vv 25–27). Together he

---

[59] Calvin, *Commentary*, 106.

[60] Dodd, *Interpretation*, 409.

[61] Brodie, *Gospel*, 470–471.

[62] Moloney, *Gospel*, 413.

> and they are now ready to rise. Thus the way is
> prepared for a surprising new development—the
> growth of the vine and its branches.[63]

Although there are a number of Johannine scholars who hold to this interpretation of the seemingly intrusive command at the close of John 14, there are also many who are very sceptical about such an approach. Beasley-Murray, for instance, calls it "implausible," since the command is one that asks for physical movement rather than psychological development, and because it is not immediately apparent how the vine and branches teaching provide a clear path by which any psychological insight brings the disciples to a higher spiritual plane.[64] The view that Jesus' call is to a higher level of psychological or spiritual insight seems most attractive to those who, on the one hand, tend to downplay the validity of historical-critical investigation of biblical texts,[65] and those who, on the other hand, focus on the need to engage the text in its received version.[66]

Transitional Movement

Similar in character to the interpretation of "Delayed Physical Movement" above, but having a different outcome in terms of the significance of the teachings in John 15, is the view put forward by

---

[63] Brodie, *Gospel*, 470–471.

[64] Beasley-Murray, *John*, 263. Brown (*John*, 582), declares this approach "farfetched and unnecessary." John W. Pryor (*John: Evangelist of the Covenant People* [Downers Grove: InterVarsity Press, 1992], 104), sees this interpretation as "unnatural", and charges it with "fail[ing] to take full account of the links between 14:30–31 and 18:1–3."

[65] Cf. John Marsh, *Saint John* (Harmondsworth, England: Penguin, 1968), 515; Bruce Milne, *The Message of John* (Downers Grove, Illinois: InterVarsity Press, 1993), 208; Lesslie Newbigin, *The Light Has Come: An Exposition of the Fourth Gospel* (Grand Rapids: Eerdmans, 1982), 169–170 ("No *physical* [emphasis his] movement from the upper room at this moment is implied"); White, *The Night He Was Betrayed*, 79.

[66] Cf. John Ashton, editor, *The Interpretation of John* (Philadelphia: Fortress, 1986), 11: "The term 'diachronic' was used by Ferdinand de Saussure in his famous *Cours de linguistique générale* (117–40) to refer to the approach of linguistic theorists chiefly interested in the *history* [emphasis his] of languages. The alternative is 'synchronic': the study of the interlocking relationships that go to make up a language at a particular point in time, ignoring the problem of how it reached that state in the first place."

Westcott. He thought the challenge to be up and gone was honestly given and correctly placed.[67] There was no need to pretend it meant anything other than what it seems to mean: at this point Jesus and his disciples begin their procession to Gethsemane. In fact, he says, "it may be said that if the command had not been acted upon some notice of the delay would have been given."[68] A very reasonable explanation of the unusual command occurring as it does, therefore, is that Jesus and the disciples left the table and the room at this point and began their trek to the Mount of Olives. Since 18:1 relates that they finally crossed the Kidron Valley after the prayer found in chapter 17, the discourse of chapters 15–16 was delivered while they walked along, probably passing through vineyards where the "vine and branches" teaching of 15:1–8 would be a most appropriate object lesson.[69] Furthermore, in this explanation, given the most probable path of Jesus and his disciples from the room where the group met for the meal toward the Mount of Olives, Jesus' prayer recorded in John 17 would likely have been offered within the Temple precincts. Since the tone of the prayer has what some describe as a "priestly"[70] quality about it, the location would fit well with the content of the last chapter of the farewell discourse.

Already in the fourth century, Chrysostom understood Jesus' command to leave in this manner.[71] He interpreted chapters 15–17 as a lengthened attempt by Jesus to further encourage the fearful disciples before the terror of his betrayal and arrest would scatter them. More recently, Haenchen,[72] Carson,[73] and Stibbe,[74] among others, have championed a similar perspective.

While the larger setting of Jerusalem and the Temple precincts would allow for such a view, there are two significant problems that militate against it. First, if the evangelist takes such pains to identify

---

[67] Westcott, *Gospel*, 187.

[68] Ibid.

[69] Consistent to this theory, Westcott entitled John 15–16 "The Discourses on the Way" (p. 196).

[70] Cf. Carson, *Gospel*, 552–553.

[71] Chrysostom, *Homilies*, 279.

[72] Ernst Haenchen, *A Commentary on the Gospel of John*, 2 (Philadelphia: Fortress, 1984), 128.

[73] Carson, *Gospel*, 479–489.

[74] Stibbe, *John's Gospel*, 26.

temporal surroundings of significance to the rest of the discourse,[75] it is very strange that there is no narrative explanation of Jesus' comment in 14:31 as these developments occur, nor any suggestion of Jesus' gestures toward either the vines of nearby vineyards or the vine emblems carved into the capstones of the Temple buildings as he expresses the thoughts of 15:1–8. Second, all of the other prayers of Jesus recorded in the Fourth Gospel are introduced with a specific set of circumstances.[76] It is out of character for this prayer, particularly with the intimacy conveyed in it, to have a setting other than the one assumed by the text as a continuation of the meeting room discourse.

Displacement Theory

For Bultmann 14:31 was the key to discerning a significant displacement in the original text of the gospel.[77] Jesus was obviously finished speaking at the end of chapter 14.[78] Furthermore, he had begun in the preceding few verses to point more specifically to his passion.[79] For that reason the words of leaving "round off the factual account of the scene; the only fitting continuation is 18:1ff."[80] That is how Bultmann thought the text should be rearranged.

But if 18:1 is meant to follow 14:31, chapters 15–17 "are left in mid-air."[81] The "unavoidable conclusion" is that these chapters have been moved from their original location. Through further investigation Bultmann decided that the original and proper structure of chapters 13–17 ought to be sketched in the following manner: the last meal (13:1–30); the farewell prayer (17); and the "farewell discourses and conversations" (13:31–35; 15–16; and 13:36–14:31, in that order).

Bernard proposed a similar rearrangement.[82] He contended that some manuscript pages had become displaced along the way, and that the discourse would not make sense until the original ordering was

---

[75] The introductory notes in chapter 13, the reference to Judas leaving into the night in 13:30, and the movement *following* the prayer in 18:1.

[76] 11:38–43; 12:20–33; 19:28–30.

[77] Bultmann, *John*, 459.

[78] See 14:25, 27.

[79] 14:28–30.

[80] Bultmann, *John*, 459.

[81] Ibid.

[82] J. H. Bernard, *The Gospel According to St. John* (Edinburgh: T & T Clark, 1928), xx, 476.

recovered. His suggestion was simply to move chapters 13:31–14:31 to a position after chapter 16. Once this is done, he said, the literary flow of the discourse is smooth and easily understood. Furthermore, in this reworking of the material, the prayer of chapter 17 retains its appropriate position, serving as the conclusion to the discourse as a whole. Jesus delivers the content of the discourses in 15:1–16:33 and 13:31–14:31. Then he calls on the disciples to rise and leave. They stand, and Jesus brings them into prayer with the words of chapter 17. Bernard believes that Jesus uses this method to help the disciples focus their minds through a kind of meditative reflection on all that they have heard.[83] After being strengthened in this manner they walk out into the night to face the dark and troubling things to come.

If, indeed, there has been a displacement of the materials of the discourse this interpretation makes sense. The great problem with such a view, however, is the simple lack of evidence. Why would centuries of interpretation and manuscript tradition confirm the arrangement of the text in its received fashion rather than either quickly adopting a revised composition of the discourse or finding clues to the original form in variant manuscript families? Without more substantive verification displacement theories lack credibility.

Multiple Sources Theory

In recent scholarship a more typical approach has been to suggest that there were likely several separate versions of Jesus' farewell speech. It may be that they were produced by different hands or at different times under various circumstances, and later edited together in their present shape. Or, possibly, they were created over time by one or more individuals who used the exhortations of Jesus to address the changing circumstances of the Christian community that gave birth to the Fourth Gospel. Whatever their differing origins, these

---

[83] Ibid., 558. Interestingly, if Augustine had been fully consistent, he would have been forced into rearranging the text of these chapters as well. He lectured that the command of Jesus in 14:31 meant exactly what it seemed to mean—the call to remove from that place "to the place where He, who had nothing in Him deserving of death, was to be delivered up to death." Augustine, "Lectures on the Gospel according to St. John," [*Nicene and Post-Nicene Fathers*, 1st Series, Vol. 7 (Grand Rapids: Eerdmans, reprinted 1978), 343]. But he never explained how it was that the discourse continued in chapter 15, with Jesus seeming to do nothing about following through on his own initiative.

separate versions were brought together clumsily,[84] carefully,[85] or strategically.[86] As Beasley-Murray says, the bulk of scholars holding to the multiple source theory recognize the validity of Bultmann's dictum that all five chapters are "fully Johannine in both content and form."[87] Because of a common theology, the parallel discourse records were allowed to stand next to one another with little internal adjustment. For that reason there was no attempt to iron out minor literary irritations, like that encountered in 14:31.

Not all are agreed, of course, as to how many sources were used in creating the present farewell discourse, or the exact manner in which to handle the mental chafing produced by these rough transitions. Schnackenburg,[88] for instance, says that a responsible solution to the problem engendered by the lack of immediate response to the command of 14:31 would be to understand that there was a "later insertion"[89] into the original form of the gospel. Thus there are only two primary sources for the farewell discourse as it stands. Brown reasons in a similar manner,[90] suggesting that "the final editor simply made the best of a difficult situation and did not seek to force a new meaning on [vs.] 31."

These five interpretations of the unusual location of Jesus' leave-taking command may be grouped into two major exegetical approaches, one which takes the text as it stands and attempts to develop consistent meaning from the given data, and the other which sees 14:31 as a disruption indicating the multi-layered history behind the final version of the gospel. The "smooth" reading of the text, as Ashton called the first approach,[91] attempts a synchronic analysis of the received version of the Fourth Gospel, supposing that the text carries a full and reasonable meaning in its existing form. Thus, whether there are multiple sources for the final redaction or not, the discourse as it stands ought to allow us to elicit a logical understanding of Jesus' words and activities as presented. This is accomplished by the "delayed physical movement," "psychological movement," and

---

[84] Cf. Schnackenburg, *John*, 90–91.

[85] Cf. Pryor, *John*, 102–106.

[86] So Painter, *Quest*, 417–435.

[87] Beasley-Murray, *John*, 224.

[88] Schnackenburg, *John*, 89.

[89] Schnackenburg, *John*, 90.

[90] Brown, *John*, 656–657.

[91] Ashton, *Studying John*, 142–148.

"transitional movement" interpretations. Each takes the text as it stands, and develops its own reason for Jesus' call to group movement from its particular reading of the discourse as a whole.

From the other perspective, a sense of the "rough" reading of the text brings scholars holding a diachronic approach to an understanding of the Fourth Gospel's development as having moved through a number of stages. In this view it is neither necessary nor inherently superior for the gospel to have a "smooth" reading in its received form. Instead, interpretive approaches that investigate "manuscript displacement" or "multiple sources theory" serve only to enhance our ability to understand and to trace the issues of growth and development in the Christian community that produced this gospel.

Ashton's challenge for a greater interaction between these two approaches,[92] noted earlier, finds some response in Segovia's recent treatment of the farewell discourse.[93] With regard to the dangling call to rise and move at the end of chapter 14 he concludes that the "command itself represents a multi-layered signal on Jesus' part to leave the safety of the supper room, to begin the impending encounter with the ruler of the world, to undertake the announced departure, and to submit to the remaining and climactic events of 'the hour.'"[94] This may indeed be the case. As a surviving transitional charge from an earlier version of the discourse it has the capacity to end the previous discussion and anticipate some new turn of events or challenges. In this way it provides a clear signal that what has preceded it is a completed literary subunit.

At the same time, because of the editorial weavings that left it in its present redactive position, it challenges the reader to anticipate something new. Brodie's idea that Jesus' call, in its present location, is an invitation for the disciples to step up to the next level of spiritual growth, as exhibited by the vine and branches teaching,[95] may press the issue too far. Nevertheless, as the discourse unfolds, two things become apparent. First, 14:31 does signal the close of a literary section. Second, the vine and branches teaching of 15:1–17 is uniquely positioned and articulated, serving as the heightened center of chiastic movement, preceded and followed by passages that mirror one

---

[92] Ashton, *Studying John*, 208.
[93] Segovia, *Farewell*, p 43–47; 283–328.
[94] Ibid., 116.
[95] Brodie, *Gospel*, 470–471.

another repetitious reflection. In this sense the command of 14:31 continues to function formally in its new setting.

Another significant problem for determining the flow of the discourse emerges near the beginning of chapter 16. In 16:5, as Jesus talks of his imminent departure, he makes this bold assertion: νῦν δὲ ὑπάγω πρὸς τὸν πέμψαντά με, καὶ οὐδεὶς ἐξ ὑμῶν ἐρωτᾷ με, Ποῦ ὑπάγεις;[96] This appears quite troubling when the same question was specifically raised by Peter just a short while earlier (13:36) in identical terms.[97] Moreover, in 14:5 Thomas challenges Jesus' departure in virtually the same manner,[98] prompting Jesus to reiterate once again his supra-temporal travel plans (14:6–7). Clearly, whatever logical flow or directed movement there might have been in the character of the discourse until this point suddenly seems to breaks down. Why, in such a moment of profound intimacy with his closest friends,[99] does Jesus ignore these forthright questions, apparently pretending they have not been asked?

Three solutions are put forward by various exegetes. The first suggestion is that of some dislocation in the text. The pages of the original manuscript are out of line, creating this problem. For Bultmann[100] and Bernard,[101] who find the entire text of the farewell discourse unfortunately jumbled, the problem is dealt with simply by placing both Peter's and Thomas' questions after Jesus' challenge. As they reconstruct the order of the dislocated passages, readjusting 13:36–14:41 to a location after 16:33, Jesus can very well say what he does in 16:5 because neither Peter nor Thomas has yet voiced that particular concern. The problem is not with the text, but with the particular version which we unfortunately have been given in the process of transmission.

Another approach is that which uses the very difficulty of this progression to point to a new level of psychological meaning. Those who read the text synchronically follow Calvin's lead when he says,

---

[96] "But now I am going to him who sent me; yet none of you asks me, 'Where are you going?'"

[97] ποῦ ὑπάγεις; ("Where are you going?").

[98] Κύριε, οὐκ οἴδαμεν ποῦ ὑπάγεις: πῶς δυνάμεθα τὴν ὁδὸν εἰδέναι; ("Lord, we do not know where you are going. How can we know the way?").

[99] Cf. 15:15.

[100] Bultmann, *Gospel*, 461, 485–486.

[101] Bernard, *Gospel*, xvi–xxx.

"The answer is easy."[102]   He articulates a psychological explanation that asserts that the disciples are, in fact, growing in their understanding of Jesus' meaning as the discourse continues its development. *"Now,"* says Jesus, near the end of his teaching, "none of you asks me, 'Where are you going?'"   Earlier, before Jesus clarified what his departure meant, Peter and Thomas were voicing exactly that concern, one that they shared with their peers. But *now* they have the additional knowledge and insight that they need in order to forego asking such questions! As Jesus had elaborated on his themes of death and the Father's mansions, they had grown in their perceptiveness. Jesus' statement in 16:5 ought to be understood as his way of confirming their growth rather than as a challenge to their intelligence.

A similar approach had been proposed by Augustine some centuries earlier.[103]   He supposed that the disciples at one time did not understand the method of Jesus' physical ascension to heaven. After he had made this clear in chapter 14 they no longer had to ask him about his destination. A modern explication of this approach is found in Dodd's analysis.[104]   He believes that the disciples actually know where Jesus is going, and that Jesus' statement of rebuke is directed toward them because they are unreasonably sad about his departure which will bring glory for himself and power through the Spirit for them.

An unusual variation on this theme, but within the same family of interpretation, is that found in Hendriksen's commentary. He believes that he is able to read the changing mood of the meal table conversation based upon clues such as this.[105]   Early in the discourse the disciples were stunned and shocked into deep sorrow by Jesus' news that he was about to leave them. They barely had enough presence of mind, at that time, to whimper out some selfish nonsense of the kind recorded as coming from the lips of Peter (13:36, 37), Thomas (14:5) and Philip (14:8). However, by the time Jesus makes his bold statement in 16:5 there is no longer any excuse for his disciples to withdraw into self-pity. Now they have all the resources necessary to understand Jesus' words and his meaning. Unfortunately,

---

[102] Calvin, *Commentary*, 137.

[103] Augustine, "Lectures," 367.

[104] C. H. Dodd, *The Interpretation of the Fourth Gospel* (Cambridge: Cambridge University Press, 1984), 412–413.

[105] Hendriksen, *Exposition*, 290.

says Hendriksen, the disciples are extremely dense and self-centered. Because of their slowness Jesus speaks these words in a mixture of anger and sorrow. His declaration is actually a "bitter complaint" regarding their human weaknesses.[106]

A third, and by far the most common explanation for Jesus' failure to acknowledge the earlier questions, is the assertion that two or more textual sources were blended without careful reflection or polish by the final editor.[107] The traditions stitched together at this point repeat the same basic farewell discourse, but they arise from divergent points of view. More than that, it appears as if someone neglected to harmonize these slightly different descriptions or variously remembered incidents. "In one form of the account the question is posed by the disciples to Jesus and the context indicates that they do not understand where he is going," says Brown. "In the other form the question is not even posed because the disciples do not sufficiently understand the import of his going away."[108]

Perhaps the best resolution to this apparent syllogistic lapse comes when the diachronic readings which identify redactional editing at work, piecing together elements of discourse that were authored at different times and possibly by different persons, and the synchronic interpretations which read the text in its received form as containing clues to interpretation are both brought together in a chiastic approach. The historical background to the present shape of the text may provide an understanding as to why these different versions of seemingly the same incidents came into being. The chiastic attention to reflexive parallelism may show how they can be read in location as elements of the discourse folding back upon itself. Certainly in the literature to date there are no other obvious solutions to the unique problems presented by the unusual movements of the Johannine farewell discourse.

---

[106] Brodie takes a similar approach. Cf., *Gospel*, 496: "...the more essential solution is that the apparent contradiction be set in the context of a spiritual reality. As mentioned earlier, it is a way of saying that the advancing disciple goes through different phases—at first eager, perhaps even overeager, to know the way, but then, as the necessity emerges for some form of dying, the eagerness is lost, and the disciple, turning sadly backwards, no longer wants to follow nor even to ask the way."

[107] So Beasley-Murray, *John*, 279; Brown, *John*, 710; Painter, *Quest*, 417; Schnackenburg, *John*, 126.

[108] Brown, *John*, 710.

CRITERION #2: THERE MUST BE CLEAR PARALLELISM
BETWEEN CHIASTIC HALVES

Blomberg's second criterion calls for the specific search for reflexive repetition in the passage. There must be clear evidence of parallelism between the first and second halves.

Indeed, all who investigate the development of John 13–17 note the many instances of words, phrases, and themes that recur. One of the most difficult challenges to a literary analysis of the farewell discourse, in fact, is its preponderance of repetitions that present themselves in a manner that appears to lack direct and focused linear progression. "The logical development and coherence of the discourses are not always immediately obvious," says Dodd. "There are many repetitions. The argument often seems to return upon itself."[109] Lussier gives a picturesque analogy. He compares the eddying of themes throughout the discourse to "the circling movements of the eagle," a "spiral" of "thoughts progressively strengthened and deepened" without "logical divisions" or "systematic developments."[110] The discourse does not always flow in measured steps.

White suggests that there are "fifteen, or perhaps seventeen, examples of this doubling back upon what has already been said."[111] For the "superficial reader," he says, it seems a "rambling, almost desultory, talk."[112] Those who approach the text with the care of close scholarship find much of the same.[113] After critical analysis, and a forthright attempt to bring some harmony and direction to the discourse material, Sloyan categorically states that "any division attempted within chapters 14–16 proves artificial"[114] because of the "repetitive" style.[115]

Brown identifies at least 25 specific instances of obviously complementary thought,[116] and finds it intriguing to note that the parallels of similar repetitious elements almost always lie on either side

---

[109] Dodd, *Interpretation*, 399.

[110] Lussier, *Christ's Farewell Discourse*, 2. Cf. Brodie, *Gospel*, 428; Brown, *John*, 589–91; Schnackenburg, *John*, 58.

[111] White, *Night*, 6.

[112] Ibid.

[113] Cf. Brown, *John*, 589–593 for a full charting of these repetitions.

[114] Sloyan, *John*, 174.

[115] Cf. also Hendriksen, *Exposition*, 260.

[116] Brown, *John*, 588–589.

of 14:31. Indeed, several larger parallel sections begin to emerge from this comparison. First, virtually all of 14:1–14 is repeated in some form in 16:16–28. Second, Jesus' teachings about the παράκλητος ("Advocate") in 14:15–26 and 16:4b–15 are very similar. Third, in the last portion of chapter 14 (verses 27–31) and again in the closing section of chapter 15 (verses 18–27) and the opening paragraph of chapter 16 (verses 1–4a) Jesus' theme is the troubling that his disciples will encounter from the world which will be countered by the peace that he provides from within. Fourth, interestingly, 15:1–8 contains virtually no words that are paralleled anywhere else in the farewell discourse.

While analyses of the movements of the Johannine farewell discourse vary, there is much agreement about the repetition that occurs between the first and second halves of the discourse. Certainly there is sufficient parallel between segments of each half to test the next of Blomberg's criteria, that of direct verbal and conceptual correspondence between parallel segments.

CRITERION #3: THERE MUST BE VERBAL AND CONCEPTUAL PARALLELISM BETWEEN HALVES

As noted already in Chapter One, the chiastic movement of John 13–17 that is developed in this study can be represented in the following manner:

A Gathering scene (Focus on unity with Jesus expressed in mutual love) 13:1–35

   B Prediction of the disciple's denial 13:36–38

      C Jesus' departure tempered by assurance of the father's power   14:1–14

         D The promise of the παράκλητος ("Advocate") 14:15–26

            E Troubling encounter with the world 14:27–31

        F The vine and branches teaching
           ("*Abide in me!*")
           producing a community of mutual
           love 15:1–17

        E₁ Troubling encounter with the world
            15:18–16:4a

        D₁ The promise of the παράκλητος ("Advocate")
            16:4b–15

        C₁ Jesus' departure tempered by assurance of the father's
            power 16:16–28

     B₁ Prediction of the disciples' denial 16:29–33

A₁ Departing prayer (Focus on unity with Jesus expressed in mutual
     love) 17:1–26

Direct verbal and conceptual parallels between the paired
segments include the following. For segments A and A₁ these verbal
parallels can be noted:

- The coming of "the hour" (13:1; 17:1).
- All things/eternal life given into his [Jesus'] hands (13:3;
  17:2,7).
- Scripture fulfilled (13:18; 17:12)
- Son glorified (13:31; 17:1, 24)
- Divine love (13:34–35; 17:26)

Conceptual parallels are also evident in a significant manner:

- Work of the devil/Satan/evil one in Judas (13:2, 27; 17:12,
  15)
- Interwoven love between Jesus and the Father now shared
  with the disciples (13:1, 34, 35; 17:23, 24, 26)
- Deliberate declaration of connection between Jesus and
  the disciples (13:8; 17:6, 10, 11, 21, 22, 23).
- Jesus' imminent departure from the disciples to the Father
  (13:1, 33; 17:5, 11)

Furthermore, the act of washing was understood as symbolic of becoming clean, holy, or sanctified.[117] Because of this, the overall theme of both the prayer in chapter 17 and the footwashing event in chapter 13 have the same purpose or intent.

For segments B and B_1, focused on predictions of betrayal, there are no direct verbal parallels. The entire theme of each segment, however, is virtually identical with its opposite in the pair. In 13:36–38 Peter has a brief dialogue with Jesus after which he asserts his full allegiance. Jesus then asks a question which challenges his confident declaration, and declares Peter's imminent denial of Jesus. In much the same way 16:29–33 begins with the disciples in conversation with Jesus, declaring their full understanding of his identity and absolute confidence in their relationship with him. Again, Jesus asks a question that challenges that boldness, and then declares that they will all leave him.

In segments C and C_1 the theme is Jesus' nearing departure coupled with a promise of the power that Jesus will give to compensate the disciples for the trauma his leaving will cause them. There are direct verbal parallels found in Jesus' statements with regard to the confidence the disciples can have in prayer (14:13, 14; 16:23, 24). At the same time there is extensive conceptual parallelism between the segments in their portrayal of the place to which Jesus is going ("my Father's house," 14:2; "I… am going to the Father," 16:28) and the troubling that will give way to patience through Jesus' peace (14:1; 16:20–23).

Segments D and D_1 offer very extensive verbal parallels, as all scholars have noted:

- "Advocate" (14:16, 25; 16:7)
- "Spirit of truth" (14:17; 16:13)
- Advocate sent (14:25; 16:7)

Beside these direct parallels there are many near-parallel allusions, as well as many conceptual parallels. These segments are very closely related in their verbal and conceptual development.

---

[117] See Richard A. Muller, "Sanctification," *International Standard Bible Encyclopedia* vol. 4, edited by Geoffrey W. Bromiley (Grand Rapids: Eerdmans, 1988): 321–331.

Segments E and E₁ are also reflexive in content, with each predominately focused on the power of the "world" (14:27, 30; 15:18, 19) that will seek to unsettle the disciples, and the greater power of the Father (14:28, 31; 15:22, 24, 26; 16:3) over the world which will provide safety and peace for the disciples.

CRITERIA #4 & #5: OBVIOUS AND SIGNIFICANT PARALLELISM BETWEEN SECTIONS

These examples show the verbal and conceptual parallelism between the reflexive pairs, as required by Blomberg's third criterion. The terms and concepts that are parallel in these sections also meet Blomberg's fourth criterion: the verbal parallelism should involve central or dominant imagery or terminology, not peripheral or trivial language. The terms and concepts listed under each section above are, indeed, the dominant materials of each section. Similarly, with regard to Blomberg's fifth criterion that the verbal and conceptual parallelisms should use words and ideas not regularly found elsewhere within the proposed chiasmus, apart from one reference to the Advocate in 15:26, and the third or middle expression of the "love command" in 15:12,[118] the vast majority of terms, phrases, and concepts that are found in parallel segments are only found in those parallel segments.

CRITERION #6: CHIASTIC SUPPORT FOUND IN MULTIPLE SETS OF PARALLELED SECTIONS

Blomberg's sixth criterion is also met in this development. Blomberg finds stronger evidence of macro-chiasm when a passage shows reflexive parallelism across the mid-section through a greater number of paired sections. In the development of John 13–17 as outlined in this study there are five sets of parallels, creating a strong chiastic movement.

---

[118] The others occur in 13:34–35 and 17:26.

CRITERION #7: CHIASTIC SEGMENTS MUST FOLLOW NATURAL BREAKS IN THE TEXT

The seventh criterion proposed by Blomberg for assessing macro-chiasm is very important. Whatever chiastic development there might be in a passage should follow from the movement of the text, and not be imposed upon it. Among scholars there are different reflections on the natural breaks in the text. Still, the outline given here makes use of all commonly understood major divisions, and is in harmony with substantial research on the less well-defined transitions, as the following summary indicates.

Most Johannine scholars agree that the Fourth Gospel, apart from the prose-poem prologue of 1:1–18 and the "second ending" epilogue of chapter 21, consists of at least two prominent sections, 1:19–12:50 and 13:1–20:31.[119] From this broad division there arise other structural approaches, but few that attempt to overlook or deny the significant shift that takes place between chapters 12 and 13.[120] Ashton summarises the "four simple but strong reasons for retaining the break at the end of chapter 12:

> (1) that chapter's particularly solemn conclusion, which rounds off what Jesus has to say to the world;
> (2) the exceptionally weighty and measured

---

[119] Dodd (*Interpretation*, 289) says: "The book naturally divides itself at the end of ch. xii. The division corresponds to that which is made in all the gospels before the beginning of the Passion-narrative. But here it is made more formal. The gospel is divided at this point virtually into two books." Cf. Brown (*Gospel*), cxxxviii–cxxxix.

Five scholars who differ from this two-part narrative analysis are Everett Harrison (*Introduction to the New Testament* [Grand Rapids: Eerdmans, 1971], 212), who uses a "travel motif" to block chapters 11–20 together as Jesus' "Last Days in Jerusalem,"; Ellis (*Genius*), whose need to find chiastic parallels forces him to begin *Part V: 12:12–21:25* in the middle of chapter 12; Mlakuzhyil (*Christocentric*, 162–164), who wishes to focus on the "Hour" of Jesus in the major "Book" of the gospel, and thus begins part two at ch. 11:1, with a "bridge section;" Staley (*The Print's First Kiss*, 66–67), who finds four separate "ministries" of Jesus in the gospel, the last of which begins at 11:1; and Barnhart (*Good Wine*, 34), who proposes a complex chiastic structure which includes "first, a quaternary or mandalic development of the chiasm, and, second, the interpretation of this Johannine structure according to a unified symbolic scheme: the seven days of the new creation."

For a survey of the literature see Jan A. duRand, *Johannine Perspectives* (Doornfontein, South Africa: Orion, 1991), 113–124.

[120] Cf. Carson, *Gospel*, 103–104.

introduction to chapter 13; (3) the change of audience
from 'the Jews' to Jesus' disciples, to which
corresponds a shift in *mood* from confrontation to
consolation and encouragement; (4) the sense of
finality signalled by the word τέλος ["end"] (not
found elsewhere, but echoed in Jesus' dying
τετέλεσται—'it is accomplished' (19:30).[121]

If, indeed, the gospel is thus divided into two major sections,
what are the themes of each? Brown popularized the terms *Book of
Signs* and *Book of Glory*[122] as appropriate appellations. Each of these
titles had antecedents: Dodd had earlier suggested the former,[123] and
Bultmann, with his emphasis on the concept of δόξα ("glory") as the
normative theme of the book, was first to give shape to the latter.[124]
These titles remain in wide use.[125]

Of course, scholars are constantly searching for more accurate
descriptive language. Recently Brodie, for instance, has presented
narrative descriptions for the contents of these two sections of the
gospel. He calls the first half "The Flow of Years" (The Life of Jesus)
(chapters 1–12), and then identifies the culmination in the second half
as "The Central Mystery" (Passover) (Chapters 13–21).[126] What
remains constant in most investigations of the Fourth Gospel is a
recognition that a new development in focus and narrative intent
begins with John 13:1, thus creating a second major section.

The major literary cues used to determine boundary points
between one section and another include the placement of editorial
comment,[127] overt changes in the setting of each new scene,[128] specific

---

[121] Ashton, *Studying John*, 149.

[122] Brown, *John 1–XII*, cxxxviii.

[123] Dodd, *Interpretation*, 290. Note also Robert Fortna, *The Gospel of
Signs: A Reconstruction of the Narrative Source Underlying the Fourth Gospel*
(Cambridge: Cambridge University Press, 1970).

[124] Bultmann, *John.*

[125] Cf. Francis J. Moloney, *The Gospel of John* (Collegeville, Minnesota:
The Liturgical Press, 1998), 23–24.

[126] Brodie, *Gospel*, 425.

[127] E.g. 13:1; 13:30b.

temporal designations that lock a particular panel to an outside frame of reference,[129] and the change in dialogue from one form of interaction to another.[130] Using these it is possible to mark the change that takes place at the beginning of the discourse as a whole. There is a deliberate effort to close the public ministry of Jesus in 12:37–50. There is a clear change in scene that takes place at 13:1. The omniscient perspective of the editor emphasises that now has come Jesus' "hour" (13:1). Further, there is a change of location from the marketplace of chapter 12 to the quiet intimacy of Jesus' private session with the disciples that extends all the way through chapters 13 through 17. Together these clues require that chapter 13 be treated either as an introductory subsection of the larger whole, or as containing the scene which gives the context out of which, in typically Johannine fashion,[131] the dialogue/monologue flow. In either case, it cannot be divorced from chapters 14–17 (or even 13:31–chapter 17).[132]

---

[128] E.g. from the scene in the public places of Jerusalem that comes to a close at the end of chapter 12 to the intimate setting of the Passover Meal that opens chapter 13. The next change in setting does not happen until the beginning of chapter 18, where Jesus and the disciples actually move from the room of the Passover Meal, journeying across the Kidron Valley to an olive grove beyond it (18:1).

[129] E.g., use of the temporal clause beginning with Ὅτε in 13:12 and 13:31; the temporal character of the participial phrase Ταῦτα εἰπὼν at the beginning of 13:21.

[130] Jean Owanga-Welo, in his 1980 unpublished Ph.D. dissertation for Emory University (*The Function and Meaning of the Footwashing in the Johannine Passion Narrative: A Structural Approach*, 171), agrees that "despite the implied spatial contiguity between chapter 13 and the rest of the Farewell Discourses, chapters 14 through 17 have quite a different unity of their own... A transition from chapter 13... is marked by the change in address, i.e., from Peter to all the disciples. We can also notice the introduction of the psychological atmosphere which points to the introduction of a new situation or theme." But Owanga-Welo has a very unique agenda, causing him to find a rather substantive break in the narrative at 13:20, and then positing that the whole of chapters 11:55–20:31 be treated as a larger literary structure (31–33).

[131] Cf. the pattern between setting and speech developed in John 3:1–15/3:16–21; 5:1–18/5:19–47; within the whole of chapters 6 and 8; and again in the movement between chapters 9/10.

[132] Brodie, *Gospel*, 443, responds to redaction analysis disjunctures: "In proposing the editorial hypothesis it is sometimes said that the text obviously reflects a variety of sources. This observation appears to be right, but that is not the issue. What is in question is whether a single author worked these many sources into a coherent unity."

No literary junctures of the type that set the boundaries of the discourse at 13:1 and 18:1 appear anywhere else in chapter 13. Hence there is no justification for removing chapter 13 from the rest of the discourse.[133] According to Schnackenburg there is mutual "dependency" and "progression" enfolding all elements from 13:1 to the end of chapter 17 in a single package.[134]

From a literary perspective, even with the insights brought to bear on these chapters by the tools of historical criticism,[135] chapter 13 belongs to the farewell discourse. The announcement of the arrival of Jesus' "hour" at 13:1 is reaffirmed in Jesus' identification of Judas as the betrayer,[136] the recurring announcement of Jesus' imminent departure throughout the discourse,[137] and the finality of the concluding prayer in chapter 17. Moreover, the discourse dialogue/monologue begins in response to the contextual activities outlined in the meal table scene of chapter 13, and there is deliberate indication that all the subsequent conversation and activity throughout chapters 13–17 take place within that singular setting.[138]

The footwashing event (13:1–20) and the entire meal scene during which it takes place (13:1–30), form the occasion that determines the content of Jesus' farewell address. The discourse itself

---

[133] Even Bultmann's reconstruction of John 13–17 requires the continued presence of 13:1–30 as an integral element of the whole (*John*, 461–463). See also Dwight Moody Smith, *The Composition and Order of the Fourth Gospel: Bultmann's Literary Theory* (New Haven & London: Yale University Press, 1984), 168–174.

[134] Schnackenburg, *John*, 33–47, 57–58.

[135] Ashton, who thinks narrative criticism has gone much too far in its often deliberate shunning of historical and redaction criticism, admits that literary and thematic analysis do offer important insights of interpretive consequence if used in tandem with honest exploration of the historical development of the text. In fact, "...it may be argued that the best practitioners of the historical critical method (the names of Bultmann and Dodd as well as the lesser-known name of Hans Windisch spring to mind) showed a keen sense of the literary qualities of the Fourth Gospel" [*Studying John*, 208].

[136] Cf. 13:27—"What you are about to do, do quickly!"

[137] E.g. 13:31 ("Now..."), 13:33, 14:25–31, 16:5–7, 16:16–19).

[138] Cf. 18:1—Ταῦτα εἰπὼν Ἰησοῦς ἐξῆλθεν σὺν τοῖς μαθηταῖς αὐτοῦ πέραν τοῦ χειμάρρου τοῦ Κεδρὼν ὅπου ἦν κῆπος, εἰς ὃν εἰσῆλθεν αὐτὸς καὶ οἱ μαθηταὶ αὐτοῦ. ("After Jesus had spoken these words, he went out with his disciples across the Kidron valley to a place where there was a garden, which he and his disciples entered.")

begins with some introductory remarks and conversation at 13:31,[139] and comes into its own in chapters 14–16. Neither the footwashing scene nor the introductory remarks that begin the meal can be taken as separate from the discourse proper. Nor, indeed, does the discourse have literary independence from these scenes. As the text has come to us, there is a symbiotic union between them.[140]

While it is apparent that John 13 belongs to the larger section of chapters 13–17, what is not as quickly evident is the point at which the conversations between Jesus and the disciples take on an overtly discursive character. As Segovia notes, there is "a great deal of disagreement with regard to the beginning of the discourse."[141] The issue is not so much whether the setting at the beginning of chapter 13 belongs in the same literary unit with the rest of chapters 14 through 17,[142] but rather the specific point at which that literary unit moves from "introduction" into the more conventional stylistics of "discourse" proper.

One unique perspective on the issue is the survey advanced by Morton and McLeman.[143] They attempt to work from an analysis of prior manuscript traditions which do not actually exist, but which they claim ability to reconstruct.[144] Using these phantom manuscripts, they identify the manner in which they suppose that the manuscripts were interlaced by one or more redactors. In this manner they find a natural break in the literary flow after 13:20. Few others, however, seem convinced. Morton and McLeman appear to be correct when they point out that a temporal movement occurs at that point.[145] Still, the shift appears to be one in which similar thoughts in a connected speech turn upon an axis, and not a complete disjunction from one thought to something altogether different.

---

[139] Cf. Johannes Schneider, *Das Evangelium nach Johannes* (Berlin: Evangelische Verlagsanstalt, 1976), 251–252. So also E. L. Smelik, *Het Evangelie naar Johannes: de Weg van het Woord* (Nijkerk, the Netherlands: Uitgeverij G. F. Callenbach N. V., 1965), 229–230.

[140] Thus Dodd, *Interpretation*, 400–401; Beasley-Murray, *John*, 223–224. Cf. also Segovia, *Farewell*, 43–47.

[141] Fernando Segovia, "The Structure, *Tendenz*, and *Sitz im Leben* of John 13:31–14:31," *Journal of Biblical Literature* 104 (1985), 476.

[142] See Culpepper, *Anatomy*, 94–95.

[143] Morton and McLeman, *Genius*.

[144] They count letters and claim ability to detect alternating manuscript sources on the basis of the similar lengths of each passage.

[145] Verse 21 begins ταῦτα εἰπὼν.

A different approach, favoured by most scholars, is that outlined by Segovia. He contends that from a literary point of view the crucial section in determining the length of the "introduction" to the farewell discourse is Jesus' opening dialogue with his disciples after Judas leaves (13:31–38). He summarizes the "four major approaches" toward the literary placement of these verses: (1) either they form a part of 13:1–30 (in which case the opening literary panel would extend through the end of chapter 13), or (2) they constitute an independent unit, or (3) they form part of 14:1–31, or (4) they represent an introduction to the entire discourse.[146] Because of the manner in which the dialogue is interrupted and interspersed throughout this passage, Segovia himself favours the third approach. He is not alone, for the great majority of scholars stand with him in assessing the passage in this manner.[147]

Two literary movements are generally noted in support of this view. First, at the end of verse 30 Judas leaves the group, signalling a change in the atmosphere of the gathering. Second, Jesus makes his announcement of the arrival of the moment of "glory" in verses 31–32.[148] Even though a similar declaration was made by the narrator at the beginning of John 13, this time it comes as a part of Jesus' personal message to his disciples. For these reasons John 13:1–30 is most often understood as the "Introduction,"[149] or the "opening dramatic scene"[150] setting the stage for the actual dialogue and monologue of the farewell discourses.[151]

---

[146] Segovia, *Farewell*, 62–64.

[147] Cf. Beasley-Murray, *John*, 223; Blank, *Gospel*, 14; Brodie, *Gospel*, 442–446; Brown, *John*, 545; Bultmann, *John*, 457–461; Deeks, *Structure*, 119; James McPolin, *John* (Wilmington, Delaware: Michael Glazier, Inc., 1979), 145–146; Leon Morris, *The Gospel according to John* (Grand Rapids: Eerdmans, 1971), 53, 65–69; Rudolf Schnackenburg, *The Gospel according to St. John* (New York: Crossroads, 1987), Vol. 3, 6; Sloyan, *John*, 165–166; C. J. Wright, *Jesus the Revelation of God: His Mission and Message According to St. John* (London: Hodder and Stoughton, 1950), 281–294. See also the examination of a number of literary approaches in the first chapter of Simoens, *La Gloire d'aimer*, 1–51.

[148] Recapitulating the cry of Jesus in 12:23 that led to the swift conclusion of the first section of the gospel.

[149] Wright, *Revelation*, 281.

[150] Dodd, *Interpretation*, 400. Brown, *John*, 545, favours simply the title, "The Meal."

[151] Relying solely on perceived chiastic elements in the literary development, Ellis has more recently proposed 13:1–32 as the opening unit of the farewell discourse section of the fourth gospel. Behind this demarcation is his

When determining where the next division in the text occurs it is important to note that there appears to be an unusual move from 13:35 to 13:36. While Peter's question in verse 36 (κύριε, ποῦ ὑπάγεις)[152] follows well from Jesus' statement in verse 33, verses 34–35 intervene in a way that breaks the flow of the thought. The new command to love may follow on Jesus' declaration of the time of glory arriving (verses 31–32) and the manner in which that event will remove the Son from the presence of both the disciples and the world (verse 33) in the sense that it gives them an identity to pursue. However, the conversation related to Peter's question in 13:36 becomes far more immediate and focused on events about to transpire, in distinction from the somewhat cryptic information offered in verses 31–35, suggesting that it functions on a different level than the preceding passage.

Thus, it is not entirely clear where the secondary divisions occur within the chapter itself. Some view 13:31–38 as a separate section from that which precedes it, noting that these verses mark the departure of Judas.[153] Yet 13:31 picks up with a reference to Judas' exit in a manner that seems to draw its short speech of Jesus into the context of that particular moment. Furthermore, while Peter's question in verse

---

desire to parallel this section with that of the prayer in chapter 17. Since the concept of δόξα figures so prominently in opening of that passage (17:1–2—δόξασόν σου τὸν υἱόν, ἵνα ὁ υἱὸς δοξάσῃ σέ,. καθὼς ἔδωκας αὐτῷ ἐξουσίαν πάσης σαρκός, ἵνα πᾶν ὃ δέδωκας αὐτῷ δώσῃ αὐτοῖς ζωὴν αἰώνιον. "After Jesus had spoken these words, he looked up to heaven and said, 'Father, the hour has come; glorify your Son so that the Son may glorify you, since you have given him authority over all people, to give eternal life to all whom you have given him.'"), Ellis needs to include the reference to δόξα found in 13:31–32 as a counterbalance to that occurring in 17:1–2. However, in this opinion he stands alone, and offers no other substantive evidence for his view.

Another interesting, though uniquely held, view of the delineation of the structure of this passage occurred in A. Q. Morton's early collaboration with G. H. C. Macgregor (*The Structure of the Fourth Gospel* [London: Oliver and Boyd, 1961]) in a "statistical analysis" of the Souter Greek text of the fourth gospel. Their conclusions required differentiating between a section of one redaction source (J₁—XI.53–XIII.35) and an editorial addition (13:36–38), before 14:1 picked up a portion of the second redaction source (J₂—XIV.1–XVI.24). Thus, the "introduction" to the discourse involves all of chapter 13 through redactory conflation.

[152] "Lord, where are you going?"

[153] For an extensive analysis of the various approaches to literary outline and divisions see Segovia, *Farewell*, 64–68.

36^{154} is an immediate reflection on Jesus' announcement in verse 33 that he is leaving soon, there is a problem with the intervening two verses. In effect the "new commandment speech" of 13:34–35 appears to be a redactive insertion, as many have noted.[155] "There are," according to Schnackenburg, "many reasons for thinking that the commandment to love was an editorial addition at this point."[156] He enumerates five:

1. The "new command" seems so centrally significant to Jesus' teaching at this point, yet it is virtually ignored as Peter immediately questions Jesus' departure destination (13:36).
2. The discourse itself, as it follows from this point, does not immediately make use of the love command theme. Instead, the "new command" reappears almost strategically only at the center of the discourse in an expanded form (15:9–17), and then again near the end of the discourse in another abbreviated version (16:27).
3. Since the epistle of I John deals with this theme of the "new command" so extensively,[157] it appears that mutual love was a major theme of discussion for the moral life of the later Johannine community.[158] This may indicate that elements of the Fourth Gospel's farewell discourse, and particularly the material related to the "new command," arise from editorial redactions brought about by one or more members of the Johannine community.[159]

---

[154] "Lord, where are you going?"

[155] Cf. Brown, *John*, 609: "Considered in itself, xiii 31–38 is obviously a composite." See also, for consideration of a changing view, Segovia, *Farewell*, 321–323.

[156] Schnackenburg, *John*, 53.

[157] E.g. I John 2:7–11; 3:11–5:5.

[158] Cf. Stephen S. Smalley, *1, 2, 3 John* (Word Biblical Commentary 51; Waco: Word, 1984), xxvi–xxviii.

[159] For an extended discussion of this possibility, see J. Wellhausen, *Das Evangelium Johannis* (Berlin: Georg Reimer, 1908), 78–80; Raymond E. Brown, *The Community of the Beloved Disciple: The Life, Loves, and Hates of an Individual Church in the New Testament Times* (New York: Paulist Press, 1979), 108, 757–759; Fernando F. Segovia, "The Theology and Provenance of John 15:1–17," *Journal of Biblical Literature* 101 (1982): 115–128.

4. Similarly, the phrase γινώσκειν ἐν ("By this… will know") in verse 35 occurs only here in the Fourth Gospel, but is found often in I John.[160]

5. "The construction used in v. 34 is striking," according to Schnackenburg,[161] and appears to be very similar to syntactical developments in 13:15 and 17:21, both of which he identifies as editorial insertions into the text.

6. Although the word πάντες ("everyone") is used in other places throughout the Fourth Gospel, its particular connotations of identifying a community over against the world in 13:35 is not typical of the gospel, and is, for the most part, the manner of its use in the epistle.

7. The heightened character of the command toward mutual love in the farewell discourse, beginning here, is analogous to the use of that theme throughout the epistle I John.

If it is true, as seems indeed to be the case, that Jesus' speech about the "new command" appears as a redactional insertion at this point, it changes the focus of 13:31–38, and appears to announce a distinction between 13:31–35 and the following verses. The "new command" thus functions as a culmination of the significance of the introductory scene, rather than as part of a transitional moment into the early elements of the discourse proper. After all, 13:1 speaks about Jesus' departure to the Father as an indication that his love for his disciples had been fully expressed. If Jesus has completed his expression of the glory of the Father in his love toward the disciples, the continuation of that glory in the world will now be dependent upon the disciples serving as the further conduit for the relationship between the Father and Jesus to find demonstration. Thus, because of the later insertion of the "new command" in verses 34–35, the theme begun in 13:1 is drawn full circle and the unity of the first section of John 13–17 is found in 13:1–35. Moreover, verse 31 specifically connects Jesus' speech about the coming of the glorification of the Son to the departure of Judas. Whatever Jesus needs to say in verses 31–35 is initiated by the fact of Judas' leaving, along with the events of the evening and next day that are set in motion by the betrayer's actions.

---

[160] E.g. 2:3, 5; 3:16, 19, 24; 4:2, 13; 5:2.

[161] Schnackenburg, *John*, 53.

Another interpretive puzzle is evident at the close of chapter 13. At the beginning of the discourse there is clear progression to its temporal and logical development: when Judas leaves the group (13:30) Jesus declares that the hour of glory has arrived (13:31–32); this, he goes on to indicate, will also be the hour of his departure (13:33). Since he will be unable to carry on with the disciples in a direct leadership role, it will be up to them to carry on in the manner they had been taught (13:34–35). Of course, impetuous Peter, in response, suddenly asks where it is that Jesus is going (13:36). In a rather cryptic response, Jesus says that his destination is hidden, but someday they would all join him there (13:36). Peter is not satisfied with what appears to be a kind of double-talk on Jesus' part, and boldly asserts his deep devotion, going so far as to state that he would never allow himself to be separated from Jesus (13:37). In a rather curt manner, Jesus turns on him with a stinging prophecy of Peter's impending duplicity (13:38). It would seem most logical that Peter would reply to Jesus' challenge, yet nothing is forthcoming from him.

Not only that, but when Jesus continues to speak in 14:1, he calls for their minds to be untroubled in a manner that seems to speak only about future assurance (14:1–3) rather than present peace of mind. Perhaps the knowledge that everything will turn out right in the end is meant to defuse undue anxiety over the troubling of the next few hours, and what each of them will be experiencing (including Peter's denials).[162] Or maybe Jesus wants to affirm that no temporary break in the disciples' relationship with him will cause a permanent disruption.[163]

However one reads it, there remains a nagging intuition that the flow of communication breaks down for a moment at this point.[164] Manuscript evidence shows that copyists in some traditions felt the need to resolve the perceived tension of the dialogue at this point by adding the phrase καὶ εἶπεν τοῖς μαθηταῖς[165] at the beginning of 14:1.[166] They noticed the inadequacy of the dialogue, and felt the

---

[162] So Schnackenburg, *John*, 58; Brown, *John*, 624–625.

[163] So Segovia, *Farewell*, 79–81.

[164] Says Stibbe, *John's Gospel*, 25: "Enigmatic speech is not lacking..." at this point and others in the discourse.

[165] "And he said to the disciples..."

[166] Manuscripts D, a, c(sy^s).

need, as Bernard says, "to soften the apparent abruptness of the words which follow."[167]

Morton and McLeman seek to explain away the difficulty by asserting that there is a change of sources at 14:1.[168] Further, they find the redactive wedding of these materials done in a way that creates a new "homiletic" unity,[169] and thus minimises any disruption the transitions might otherwise cause. In their estimation, Jesus' words in 14:1 are indeed intended to serve as a response to whatever troubling Peter and the others might have experienced because of the stark revelations at the end of chapter 13. Since Peter does not come back with a further question or challenge, it is obvious that Jesus' words were sufficient.

Bultmann also thinks there is a change of source material at 14:1. He does not however, find the given text difficult. He believes that since the Evangelist has a specific point to make (i.e., comfort for a tested faith), the final literary creation, "in the language of myth," makes perfect sense in its received form.[170] Most scholars agree with him that although this apparent incongruity fosters a moment of stumbling within the logical flow of the discussion, it is not without reasonable explanation.

Whether the discourses proper begin at 13:31 or 14:1, there is general recognition that the dialogue/monologue of Jesus following the "introductory" setting and continuing through the end of chapter 16 has a focused literary purpose.[171] On the one hand, it serves as a "last will and testament."[172] Jesus knows that he is about to die, and he wishes to offer a reflective word about these times and their significance to the small group of people who had a very special relationship with him. On the other hand, these discourses serve, in the Fourth Gospel, broadly, both philosophically and theologically, to reflect upon the fulfillment of Jesus' glorification that will soon be accomplished by way of his return to the Father. In addition, these farewell discourses function as a revelatory prelude to the passion. Jesus needs to explain the meaning of his death in a way

---

[167] Bernard, *Gospel*, 530.

[168] A. Q. Morton and J. McLeman, *The Genesis of John* (Edinburgh: Saint Andrew Press, 1980), 50–53.

[169] Ibid., 203–204.

[170] Bultmann, *John*, 457–461, 595–597.

[171] Cf. Raymond F. Collins, *These Things Have Been Written: Studies on the Fourth Gospel* (Grand Rapids: Eerdmans, 1990), 89–90.

[172] So Brown, *John*, 582

that gives his disciples hope instead of sorrow, and which elevates the act of his demise into something actively redemptive rather than passively tragic.[173]

Chapter 14, although connected to what precedes it, has a strong cohesive unity in and of itself, with verse 1 marking the start of a more explicit exhortation on the part of Jesus. It is universally recognised that Jesus' prediction of Peter's denial in 13:38 is not directly connected to the theme of comfort that begins at 14:1. Most perceive editorial redaction in the closing verses of chapter 13,[174] creating an intentional note of darkness[175] that will be picked up again in its parallel in 16:29–33.[176] In fact, it appears that the comforting promises of 14:1–4 are intended as a response to the trauma developing because of Jesus' dour prediction in much the same way as 16:16–28 provides similar assurance in the face of a broader defection.

The next issue of literary development occurs in the transition from 14:11 to 14:12, which might or might not signal the beginning of a new literary segment. On the one hand, there is a type of conclusion drawn in 14:11 by the use of the same form of πιστεύετε[177] (either active indicative or active imperative) that Jesus spoke earlier in 14:1. Jesus has called for trust (14:1) in response to his leaving (13:36–38), and rooted that trust in both a future expectation (14:2–4) and a shared divine identity between the Father and the Son (14:5–10). The challenge to trust is reiterated negatively in verse 10, and here in verse 11 put forward in the same positive way as 14:1, possibly bringing this matter to a conclusion. However, verse 12 seems to continue addressing the theme of trust, but now speaking of the πιστεύων,[178] which moves the conversation into a new dimension. Second, 14:12 begins with a double ἀμὴν[179] statement. These occur 25 times in the Fourth Gospel, thirteen times with an introductory editorial comment[180] (such as "Jesus answered," or "then Jesus said"), and

---

[173] Cf. Bultmann, *John*, 457–461; Segovia, *Farewell*, 2–20.

[174] Cf. Brown, *John*, 616.

[175] Beasley-Murray, *John*, 248.

[176] Schnackenburg, *John*, 164.

[177] "believe me."

[178] "the one who believes."

[179] "truly."

[180] 1:51; 3:3; 3:5; 5:19; 6:26; 6:32; 6:53; 8:34; 8:58; 10:7; 13:21; 13:38; 16:23.

twelve times without,[181] including here. Whenever ἀμὴν ἀμὴν
λέγω ὑμῖν[182] occurs with the introductory editorial comment, it
functions to continue the thought of the passage and never signals the
beginning of a new pericope. However, sometimes when, as here,
there is no introductory editorial comment, the statement may indicate
either the start of a new thought[183] or a summary point that stands
somewhat alone,[184] distinct in measure from the flow of its preceding
context. The exact nature of its implication for the flow of this passage
is ambiguous, and most exegetes make the connection with the
preceding verses fairly strong.

It is commonly held that 14:15 opens a new topic of the
monologue. While there is a connection here to 14:12–13 based on the
idea of doing works, there is, at the same time, a new direction to the
thought. In the preceding verses there is emphasis on the display of
visible activity;[185] after this point the tenor of Jesus' discourse shifts to
"obedience."[186] Not only that, but 14:16 introduces the concept of the
παράκλητος ("Advocate") for the first time.

There appears to be a kind of summation at the end of 14:24:
καὶ ὁ λόγος ὃν ἀκούετε οὐκ ἔστιν ἐμὸς ἀλλὰ τοῦ
πέμψαντός με πατρός.[187] Indeed, 14:25 begins with ταῦτα
λελάληκα ὑμῖν,[188] a phrase which occurs only six times in the
Fourth Gospel,[189] all within the farewell discourse. At least half of the
occurrences signal the start of a new thought or instruction. In fact,
while 14:25–27 pick up on several themes already addressed,[190] they
do so as a kind of introduction to Jesus' encounter with the world
(14:30–31).

---

[181] 3:11; 5:24; 5:25; 6:47; 8:51; 10:1; 12:24; 13:16; 13:20; 14:12;
16:20; 21:18.

[182] "Very truly, I tell you…"

[183] E.g., 5:24; 10:1.

[184] E.g., 5:25; 6:47.

[185] "Making works" (τὰ ἔργα...ποιῶ).

[186] Ἐὰν ἀγαπᾶτέ με, τὰς ἐντολὰς τὰς ἐμὰς τηρήσετε: ("If you
love me, you will keep my commandments.")

[187] "…and the word that you hear is not mine, but is from the Father who
sent me."

[188] "I have said these things to you…"

[189] 14:25; 15:11; 16:1, 4, 6, 33.

[190] The παράκλητος ("Advocate"), peace, and untroubled hearts.

Even with these smaller divisions there is a great cohesiveness to the whole of chapter 14. Noting the overall unity of John 14, Brown identifies the whole chapter as "Division 1" of the extended discourse[191] that has been introduced by the events and dialogue of chapter 13. In spite of the fact that, as Brodie indicates, "the dividing of chap. 14 is unusually difficult,"[192] most scholars see a significant literary shift between verses 14 and 15.[193] There are three primary reasons to respect this literary division. First, from 13:36–14:14 the discourse exhibits a dialogic character in which Peter (13:36), Thomas (14:5), and Philip (14:8) in rapid succession each ask a question. Jesus immediately responds to these questions, but in 14:15 appears to begin a more monologic form of discourse. There will be other questions from among the disciples,[194] but not again in the manner of giving fundamental direction to Jesus' teaching.

Second, there is a shift in focus between 14:1–14 and the verses following. Beasley-Murray identifies it as the movement from talk about the character of Jesus as revealed by his actions and activities in the past with the disciples, to promises of things to come in the near and distant future.[195] Whereas they have received from Jesus enough to provide them with the knowledge necessary to be on intimate terms with him (14:1–14), they will now also need to receive some assurance of his presence and power with and for them in the troubling days ahead (14:15–31).

Third, Jesus' statements in 14:15 and 14:16 are tied together by the conjunction κἀγώ,[196] and 14:16 contains the first of five "Paraclete passages"[197] which focus specifically on the coming and ministry of the παράκλητος.[198] This shows the turn to a new subject of discourse at 14:15.

Another minor but distinctive literary movement happens between 14:26 and 14:27. In 14:25–26 Jesus completes the thought begun in 14:15–16. In the former verses he announced the coming of

---

[191] Brown, *John*, 623.

[192] Brodie, *Gospel*, 458; cf. Brown, *John*, 623: "The internal organization of ch. xiv is not easy to discern"; Schnackenburg, *John*, 58.

[193] Cf. Bultmann, *John*, 473; Brown, *John*, 623; Beasley-Murray, *John*, 244–245.

[194] Judas in 14:22 and the group as a whole in 16:18 and 16:29.

[195] Beasley-Murray, *John*, 244–245.

[196] "…and I…"

[197] 14:16–17; 14:26; 15:26; 16:7–11; 16:12–15.

[198] "Advocate."

the παράκλητος and in the latter verses he reiterates that promise. In between he identifies the manner in which the παράκλητος will function, drawing attention to the union created by the παράκλητος between himself, the Father and the disciples. This theme points ahead to the thesis of the vine and branches teaching of 15:1–17 where the idea is explored in a representational way for the discourse as a whole.

With the παράκλητος teaching of 14:15–26 in place Jesus brings this section of the farewell discourse to a conclusion with what Beasley-Murray calls an "epilogue."[199] Here the teachings that began the first part of the discourse return, most notably the injunction "do not let your hearts be troubled" (14:1; 14:27). This culmination of the beginning section of the discourse reaches an abrupt conclusion when Jesus declares, in 14:31, "Arise; let us leave!"[200]

From this analysis the following divisions emerge as the primary literary sections in John 13–14:

- The gathering scene   13:1–35
- Prediction of the disciple's denial   13:36–38
- Jesus' departure tempered by the assurance of the father's power   14:1–14
- The promise of the παράκλητος ("Advocate")   14:15–26
- Troubling encounter with the world   14:27–31

Moving on to chapter 15, there is general agreement that 15:1–8 forms the nucleus of the next literary unit. These verses pointedly state (15:1, 15:5a), extend (15:2, 6), and apply (15:3–4, 5b, 7–8) the metaphor of the vine, branches, and caretaker. And, except for a reference to "bearing fruit" in 15:16, the metaphor is finished at verse 8.

What is less held in agreement is the length of the section that begins with 15:1–8. Bernard, for instance believes that 15:1–8 should be understood as a separate section from what follows. He points to the phrase "As the Father has loved me, so have I loved you," which opens verse 9,[201] and sees it as signalling the beginning of a new idea just as a similar phrase did in 13:2. In fact, there is even a rather clear parallel between 15:9–17 and 13:34–36, with the verses in chapter 15

---

[199] Beasley-Murray, *John*, 262–264.

[200] Ἐγείρεσθε, ἄγωμεν ἐντεῦθεν.

[201] Bernard, *Good Wine*, 483.

broadening the ideas stated in seminal form earlier. Thus, a new idea, repeated and expanded upon from chapter 13, begins here at 15:9. In this manner Bernard sees 15:1–8 standing alone.

Westcott believes otherwise. He sees 15:1–10 as the first of seven "discourses on the way."[202] Its theme is "The Living Union" between Jesus and his disciples, and is developed in five smaller units of two verses each.[203]   Schnackenburg,[204] Hendriksen,[205] and Newbigin[206] would extend the opening pericope of chapter 15 one verse further, and make the break between literary units at verse 12, where "Jesus now proceeds... from the precept 'Abide in me' (15:1–11)... to the next one, 'love one another.'"[207]

Several scholars, such as Morris[208] and Tasker,[209] draw the line after verse 16, when the final reference to the vine imagery has been made. Morris "hesitantly" opts for the break before verse 17 rather than after it, because he sees the command to love as "attracting the persecution of the world."[210]   That, of course, would tie verse 17 to what follows.

Most often, however, 15:1–17 is understood to be a single literary unit.[211] Brown notes two reasons for this: "The last mention of the imagery of vine ('bear fruit') appears in 16, and there does seem to be a change of subject between 17 and 18."[212] The change he refers to is one of verbal mood: from the imperative command to love to the

---

[202] Westcott, *Gospel*, 196–197.

[203] Similarly Beasley-Murray, *John*, 269.

[204] Schnackenburg, *John*, 96.

[205] Hendriksen, *Exposition*, 293–294.

[206] Newbigin, *Light*, 195–196.

[207] Hendriksen, *Exposition*, 305.

[208] Morris, *Gospel*, 668–669.

[209] Tasker, *Gospel*, 173–174.

[210] Morris, *John*, 677.

[211] Cf. Brown (*John*, 665): "Generally xv 1–17 is recognised by scholars to be a unit." Segovia (*Farewell*, 125): "The most frequent position, the designation of 15:17 as a major break in these chapters and the corresponding identification of 15:1–17 as the first unit of discourse within John 15–16, is based on two critical observations. First, the figure of the vine, introduced and developed within 15:1–8, reappears in 15:16, which in turn forms part of the ongoing development of the theme of love in 15:9–17.   Second, as opposed to the immediately following discourse material beginning with 15:18, 15:1–17 focuses on the internal affairs of the community, on the proper relationship of the disciples to Jesus and one another."

[212] Brown, *John*, 677.

indicative warning of hatred. Bultmann[213] suggests a further reason for considering 15:1–17 as a literary whole, namely the recurring emphasis on the word "abide" throughout the passage. These repeated expressions hold the larger unit together in a single pericope. Most scholars agree with this analysis.[214]

Still, within this larger unit, smaller subsections are noted. Segovia[215] describes four different approaches to the further analysis of 15:1–17, with one dominating the field. "The majority position argues for a twofold division of these verses with a break at 15:8…"[216] Most thorough in his explication of this approach is Bultmann, who finds structural parallelism between verses 1–8 and 9–17.[217] The first section is built around the theme "abide in me," while the latter calls for the disciples to "abide in my love. "

Schnackenburg gives shape to the first of Segovia's "minority positions," placing the literary shift after verse 11.[218] He believes the opening subsection (vs. 1–11) appeared originally as a *"mashal"* in a narrative context. Lifted from that former existence and embellished, it now functions as the lead to a second, similar literary subunit (vs. 12–17) with "paraenetic" emphasis for the Eucharistic celebrations of an early Christian community.[219]

Brown's approach forms the next "minority position." In his understanding of this passage, 15:1–6 declares the "figure" of the vine and branches, while 15:7–17 explains that figure "in the context of the Last Discourse themes."[220] Further, Brown sees inclusion in each of these two sections, and goes on to identify the development of the latter unit in chiastic form.

A remaining approach opts for a threefold division, with a first break either at 15:6[221] or 15:8[222] and the second after verse 11. In this

---

[213] Bultmann, *John*, 532–541.

[214] Barrett, *Gospel*, 470; Beasley-Murray, *John*, 269; Brodie, *Gospel*, 475; Schnackenburg, *John*, 95–96; Segovia, *Farewell*, 125–126.

[215] Segovia, ibid., 127–131.

[216] Ibid., 127.

[217] Bultmann, *John*, 529, 539–540.

[218] Schnackenburg, *John*, 108.

[219] A minor variation is found in Brodie, *Gospel*, 475–479, where the ταῦτα of verse 11 signals the beginning of the hortatory response to the vine and branches teaching metaphor.

[220] Brown, *John*, 665–666.

[221] Bernard, *Good Wine*, 477–485.

[222] Mlakuzhyil, *Christocentric*, 225.

delineation the respective sections focus thematically on the vine and branches image, the divine love link, and finally the mutual love link.

It is clear, from the preceding, that there is a significant majority of interpretive scholarship that holds to a two-part analysis of 15:1–17 with the transition from one sub-section to the next taking place after verse 8. In addition, these scholars also tend to agree on the following exegetical insights:

1. All affirm that there is a profound literary break between 14:31 and 15:1 signalled by the command of Jesus for the group to rise and leave. This break is further indicated by the change in topic and discourse style between the sections on either side of the chapter divide.
2. Virtually all are certain that another significant break happens after 15:17.
3. Further, the perspective is held almost unanimously that a significant shift occurs following verse 8. Brown[223] alone breaks the pericope after verse 6, basing his analysis on two elements: verses 1–6 have no allusions to "last supper themes," while verses 7–17 have many; and there appears to be, in his estimation, a rather sophisticated chiastic structure tying together the words and phrases of verses 7–17.
4. Finally, there is common agreement that the vine and branches teaching of 15:1–8 is unique within the larger discourse material of chapters 13–17. Nowhere else in the discourse does Jesus use similar analogies to impersonal objects when explaining his relationship with his disciples. Nor are the metaphors of vine and branches parallel with any comparable teaching in these chapters.

Several conclusions may be drawn from this survey. First, the initial discourse section is brought to a definitive end by means of the unusual command of Jesus in 14:31. Second, 15:9–17 holds a closer relationship to 15:1–8 than it does to the material that follows it, with a strong possibility, following Schnackenburg,[224] that verses 9–11 are more strongly linked to the vine and branches teaching than are

---

[223] Brown, *John,* 665–666.
[224] Schnackenburg, *John,* 91–93.

verses 12–17.[225]   Third, a new section of discourse material begins again at 15:18.

It is generally held that the section that begins at 15:18 extends through the first part of 16:4. Also, most scholars recognise that the final sentence in 16:4 belongs to the paragraphs that follow rather than those that precede it. There are two reasons for this perspective. First, the initial sentence in 16:4 is a summation, closing off the discussion of the previous verses. Second, verse 5 begins with νῦν,[226] responding to the temporal reference in the last part of verse 4.[227] Thus, a new development begins at 16:4b.

There appears to be a clear break between 16:15 and 16:16. The former verse concludes Jesus' thought on the coming of the Spirit, while the latter begins again the theme of Jesus' imminent departure, carrying on that conversation through to verse 28.

There is a kind of concluding quality about 16:29–33. On the one hand, the disciples seem to react positively to the discourse as it has taken place (verses 29–30). On the other hand, Jesus uses his stock discourse phrase[228] to review several main points (verse 33). And in between (verses 31–32) there is a statement regarding the coming time of denial and desertion by the entire group that echoes Jesus' harsh words to Peter in 13:38.

Most scholars view the rest of chapter 16 (16:4b–33) as having been authored in a singular creative moment. Painter calls this section the "third version" of the discourse, reflecting, in his view of the history of the development of the text, a time when the Johannine community had become totally separated from its Jewish beginnings and the synagogue in which conflict had first erupted over the issue of Jesus' messianic claims.[229]

Brown,[230] Carson,[231] and Schnackenburg[232] see 16:4b–15 as the first sub-unit within this larger section. Segovia notes that there are

---

[225] Because of the five-times recurrence of "abide in me" (μείνατε ἐν ἐμοί) or its variations in these verses, carrying along the major theme of verses 1–8.

[226] "now."

[227] Ταῦτα δὲ ὑμῖν ἐξ ἀρχῆς οὐκ εἶπον, ὅτι μεθ' ὑμῶν ἤμην. ("I did not say these things to you from the beginning, because I was with you.").

[228] ταῦτα λελάληκα ὑμῖν παρ' ὑμῖν. ("I have said this to you...").

[229] Painter, *Quest*, 428–432.

[230] Brown, *John*, 703.

[231] Carson, *John*, 532–542.

[232] Schnackenburg, *John*, 125.

three primary reasons for assessing a break between verses 15 and 16.[233]   First, there is a dominant focus in 16:4b–15 on the παράκλητος ("Advocate") which does not resurface again after verse 15.   Second, the verses following 16:15 pick up themes that were initiated early in the discourse,[234] but which did not take a prominent place in chapter 15. Third, in 16:17–19 and 16:29–31 the monologic character of the discourse, which had been present since 14:27, is again interrupted by small segments of dialogue.

Determining the next literary break following that between 16:15 and 16:16 is more difficult. An interesting clue to help in the analysis is found at the beginning of 16:28. The best manuscripts, including Sinaiticus and Vaticanus, support the existence and position of ἐξῆλθον παρὰ τοῦ πατρός[235] at the beginning of the verse, while a small family of Western manuscripts omits them.[236] Carson[237] and Brown[238] note that the transition from verse 27 to verse 28 would be smoother without the clause, eliminating the virtual repetition of the last clause of verse 27.   The strength of the manuscript evidence supporting the clause in its present location, however, mitigates against its removal. With that in mind, it appears that the repetition between the final clause of verse 27 and that at the beginning of verse 28 signals a unique role for the content of verse 28. Brown notes that there is a very striking chiasm evident in the verse as it stands:

> ἐξῆλθον παρὰ τοῦ πατρὸς
> καὶ ἐλήλυθα εἰς τὸν κόσμον·
> πάλιν ἀφίημι τὸν κόσμον
> καὶ πορεύομαι πρὸς τὸν πατέρα.[239]

---

[233] Segovia, *Farewell*, 215–216.
[234] Jesus' imminent departure, promise of the Father's power, predictions of disciples' denials.
[235] "I came from the Father…"
[236] D, W, b, ff², syˢ, ac², pbo.
[237] Carson, *John*, 550.
[238] Brown, *John*, 724–725.
[239] "I came from the Father
    and have come into the world;
    again, I am leaving the world
    and I am going to the Father."

This deliberately crafted declaration thus appears to be a concluding statement to the leave-taking thrust of Jesus' speech in 16:16ff. Not only so, but the confident rejoinder of the disciples in verse 29 seems to cause Jesus to address a new theme, that of their common desertion (16:31–32). Brodie further supports this division between 16:28 and 16:29 when he points to λέγουσιν[240] as the opening word of 16:29, noting that some form of the word often signals the beginning of a new literary section.[241]

The last section of the discourse is recognized universally as consisting in the prayer of John 17. While Jesus' prayer in chapter 17 is not an entirely seamless garment, as some have suggested,[242] it has an inner cohesiveness that makes a reduction of the prayer into sub-units very difficult.[243] It appears to be woven from a single strand of thought,[244] giving some the impression that it was created by the Johannine community as a reflection on the content of chapter 13, and used in the Eucharistic rites of the early church.[245]

Most scholars identify the prominent points of movement in the text as those that mark the transition from personal to communal focus at verse 6, and that which again broadens the focus to catholic expansion at verse 20.[246] Brown calls this prayer "one of the most majestic moments in the Fourth Gospel,"[247] and a natural "climax" to the last discourse in the manner of Moses' prayer at the close of Deuteronomy. Even Bultmann, who juggles various elements of the text of John 13–17 in hopes of finding an "original" order, does not argue against the integrity of the prayer as a single unit. While he acknowledges that elements of the prayer have origins prior to the "Evangelist," he is also sensitive to the well-crafted nature of the final form in its wholeness.[248]

---

[240] "[His disciples] said…"

[241] Brodie, *Gospel*, 501.

[242] Cf. Hendriksen, *Exposition*, 307.

[243] Cf. Schnackenburg, *John*, 167–169.

[244] Cf. M. J. J. Menken, *Numerical Literary Techniques in John: The Fourth Evangelist's Use of Numbers of Words and Syllables* (Leiden: E. J. Brill, 1985), 229–230.

[245] Ibid., 168.

[246] Haenchen (*Commentary*, 158) says that "the lines of demarcation among verses 1–5 (others prefer to say vv 1–8), 9–19, and the remainder are in reality not so evident as it might appear; the unity of the passage prevails by far."

[247] Brown, *John*, 744.

[248] Bultmann, *John*, 849.

Similarly, Schnackenburg, who discovers in the prayer of John 17 a remarkable "new composition,"[249] is only moderately willing to talk about verse 3 as "an additional gloss"[250] and verses 20–21 as "a second supplement."[251] "Even if we regard vv. 20f as an early addition by a second author," he says, "at least from the literary point of view, these two verses are, from the theological point of view, not alien to the passage as a whole and they have to be explained in the light of Jn 17."[252] In fact, he asserts elsewhere, the prayer of John 17 "forms a complete unity in itself."[253]

There are no clear parallels to this prayer in the rest of the New Testament. Scholars have ranged expansively in search of similar forms of literature elsewhere,[254] yet the outcome tends to collect around three types of modest proposals. First, those who hold that the literary genre of the John 13–17 is a standardized "Farewell Discourse"[255] see the prayer as an addition by the final redactor, possibly in imitation of the song of Moses near the end of Deuteronomy.[256] Others, secondly, such as Dodd[257] and Bultmann,[258] find similarities between John 17 and the hymnic prayers found in the Hermetic writings or the Gnostic Mandaean literature of Egyptian origins.

A third approach is taken by Brodie, who finds a striking affinity between the prayer of John 17 and the poetic prologue that opens the Fourth Gospel.[259] If that lyrical introduction to the gospel had antecedents, perhaps the prayer that concludes the farewell discourse was also developed out of a "canticle" that may have existed in an earlier form in Jewish or Christian liturgies. Since the Passover meal normally ended with the Hallel,[260] some suggest that the prayer of John

---

[249] Schnackenburg, *John*, 167.

[250] Ibid., 169, 172–173.

[251] Ibid., 169, 188–189.

[252] Ibid., 189.

[253] Ibid., 91.

[254] Cf. Schnackenburg, *John*, 197–200.

[255] Cf. Segovia, *Farewell*, 5–20.

[256] Brown, *John*, 744–748.

[257] Dodd, *Interpretation*, 420–423.

[258] Bultmann, *John*, 490.

[259] Brodie, *Gospel*, 508–511.

[260] "Hallel" is the designation of several groups of Psalms that express praise to God ("Hallelujah" means "Praise Yahweh"). Psalms 113 and 114 were typically sung before the Passover feast, and Psalms 115–118 after the drinking of the last cup of the Passover meal. Cf. Mark 14:26.

17 is a literary creation designed to transform the theocentric praise of the Hallel into a Christocentric hymn for the early church's eucharistic celebration.[261] In fact, when Bultmann transposes the prayer to the beginning of the farewell discourse, he even goes so far as to assert that it replaces the sacramental institution so strikingly missing from the Fourth Gospel.[262]

However one understands the character of the prayer of John 17, perspectives such as those stated above are, as Brown notes, often "highly romantic," and often "quite incapable of proof."[263] Although there is some dispute about the literary precedents and character of the prayer, there is widespread agreement regarding its function in the larger discourse, particularly among those who allow it to stand in its present location. Already in the fifth century, Cyril of Alexandria spoke of Jesus here as a "high priest" making intercession for his people.[264] David Chyrträus, an early Lutheran scholar (1531–1600), was first to designate this passage as Jesus' "high priestly prayer."[265] Today that appellation is widely used.[266] As the hour of glory unfolds, Jesus stands like a priest between heaven and earth, binding his followers to the Father's heart.

Yet, since a high priest stands between earth and heaven, between humanity and deity, and addresses each, there are differing views as to the primary focus of this prayer. Some emphasise the intercessory nature of the prayer,[267] saying that Jesus petitions the Father to fulfil the divine revelation of glory through the Son (17:1,5)

---

[261] Oscar Cullman, *Early Christian Worship* (London: SCM, 1953); Joachim Jeremias, *The Eucharistic Words of Jesus* (Philadelphia: Fortress, 1966), 89–96.

[262] Bultmann, *John*, 485–486. Cf. also Schnackenburg, *John*, 42–47.

[263] Brown, *John*, 746.

[264] Dodd, *Interpretation*, 419.

[265] *De morte et vita aeterna* (1581). Cf. S. C. Agourides, "The 'High-Priestly Prayer' of Jesus," *Studia Evangelica 4* (1968): 137–143.

[266] Cf. Beasley-Murray, *John*, 293–294; Brown, *John*, 750; Haenchen, *John*, 147; Morris, *John*, 716; Schnackenburg, *John*, 168; Sloyan, *John*, 196; Westcott, *Gospel*, 197. Still, as Schnackenburg (*ibid.*, 201) notes, such a title "is only partly justified and to some extent misleading," since Jesus has not yet left earth to take up a permanent position in the universal temple referred to in Hebrews 4:14–5:10; 7:1–10:39; 12:18–24; 13:11–16. Westcott (*Gospel*, 238) says the more proper terminology would be "the Lord's Prayer." Cf. also Barrett (*Gospel*, 500): "...the common description of it as the 'High-priestly prayer'... does not do justice to the full range of material contained in it."

[267] So, e.g., Schnackenburg, *John*, 167–168; White, *Night*, 122–123.

and further to maintain a revelatory presence with the disciples (17:10–11, 15, 17–18, 23). Others focus on the exaltation of the Son that happens in this "hour,"[268] and see Jesus' primary intent as one of "consecrating" the disciples for presentation to the one above.[269]

Dodd takes the mediatorial role of Jesus a step further, and characterises John 17 as the Johannine version of Jesus' "ascension" to the Father.[270] Building on this idea, and pressing it to its theological conclusion, Käsemann believes that chapter 17 is the interpretive key to the whole of the Fourth Gospel. Its portrayal of the "epiphany and presence of glory," he says, serves as an esoteric reminder of the meaning of redemption and Christian unity for a struggling faith community at the end of the first century.[271]

Because of the specific mediatorial role in which Jesus portrays himself as he expresses the prayer of John 17 virtually all interpretive approaches which allow the text to stand as it has been received view this chapter as a conclusion to the discourse materials proper. It forms the "climax"[272] or "culmination"[273] of the broader literary unit (chapters 13–17), gathering the themes of the discourse into a resounding crescendo-like finale. Every line of the prayer echoes with thoughts and theses previously probed:

- the arrival of "the hour" (17:1—13:1,13)
- the "glorification of the Son and the Father (17:2,4–5,10,24—13:31–32; 15:8)
- assertion of the "authority" of the Son (17:2—13:3,8,13–17,34; 14:14–15,21,24; 15:10–17,20; 16:23–24)
- "life" as knowledge of the Father through Jesus (17:3—13:1; 14:1,6–10,20,23; 15:1–17)
- Jesus revealing the Father (17:6—14:6–10)
- the divine election of the disciples (17:6—13:18; 15:16,19)

---

[268] For Bultmann, the mention of the "hour" in the opening sentence of the prayer is the key to its location and interpretation: "The first petition is in fact its whole contents" (*John*, 490).

[269] Cf. Brodie, *Gospel*, 505–506.

[270] Dodd, *Interpretation*, 419.

[271] Käsemann, *The Testament of Jesus: A Study of the Gospel of John in the Light of Chapter 17* (London: SCM, 1968).

[272] So Brown, *Gospel*, 744; Schnackenburg *John*, 167.

[273] So Dodd, *Interpretation*, 419.

- the return of Jesus to the Father (17:11,13—13:1,33; 14:2–3,12,28; 15:26; 16:7,10,17, 28)
- power found in the divine name (17:11—14:13–14; 16:24)
- the betrayal of Judas (17:12—13:18–30)
- joy for the disciples (17:13—16:19–24)
- the "hatred" of the "world" toward the disciples (17:14,16—14:27; 15:18–25; 16:1–4, 8–9,11,33)
- "sanctification" (17:17–19—13:2–10; 15:3)
- the witness of the disciples (17:20—15:20,27)
- the unity of the disciples (17:21–23—13:34–35; 15:12–14,17)
- the Father "in" the Son and the disciples (17:23—13:31–32; 14:9–11,20,23; 15:4–7,9–11; 16:32)
- eschatological reunion (17:24—13:36; 14:2–3,28)
- the inability of the world to "know" the Father (17:25—14:17,22; 15:18–19)
- Jesus as "sent" by the Father (17:25—13:20; 14:24,31; 15:10,21; 16:5,27–28)
- the continued revelation (17:26—14:16–17,26; 15:26; 16:7–15)
- the ultimacy of love (17: 26—13:1,34–35; 14:21,23–24; 15:9–17; 16:27)

Clearly there are thematic and literary links between the prayer and what precedes it throughout the discourse. It is also obvious that the prayer has great internal unity,[274] although assessing its structural components is quite challenging.[275]

An early contribution to theories of literary design was offered by Westcott, whose three-fold division of the ever-broadening circles of petitioning (Jesus for himself, 17:1–5; for his disciples, 17:6–19; and for the whole church, 17:20–26)[276] is still widely used.[277] There are some variations on this theme.[278] Brown, for instance, recognizes the transitional character of verses 6–8, and

---

[274] Cf. Haenchen, *John*, 158.

[275] Cf. Morris (*John*, 716): "The prayer is difficult to subdivide for it is essentially a unity. However it is possible to discern a movement."

[276] Westcott, *Gospel*, 240.

[277] Cf. Brodie, *Gospel*, 580; Bultmann, *John*, 490–522; Marsh, *John*, 553; Schnackenburg, *John*, 167–168.

[278] Cf. Menken, *Literary Techniques*, 230–238.

includes them in the first literary subunit, thus providing a better poetic balance to his analysis of the chapter as a whole.[279] Others separate these three verses (6–8) from either the prior or following subunits, and form with them a fourth literary division.[280] Still others perceive the transitional movements from one grouping to the next in slightly different locations, beginning new sections at verses 1b, 6, 20, and 24.[281] Malatesta, in a rather extensive analysis,[282] identifies five unique literary subunits (1–5, 6–8, 9–19, 20–24, and 25–26) that fold together in chiastic parallelism.

Still, the variety of assessments of the prayer's internal structure do little to alter scholars' views on its obvious place in the thematic development of the farewell discourse materials. Schnackenburg speaks for most contemporary scholarship when he asserts the role chapter 17 holds for the movement of the discourse in its given location:

> In the present configuration of the gospel, there is no more suitable place for this prayer and there would also be no better place in a possible original form of the gospel. It would also be out of the question to place it in front of the farewell discourse in Chapter 14 (that is, between 13:30 and 31), because such a climax has to occur at the end of all the discourses.[283]

As a final expression of the themes of the discourse, the prayer of chapter 17 projects a dramatic climax to Jesus' intimate portrait of "oneness" among the Father, the Son and the disciples. In this way the context is fully set for the passion story that follows, since the "hour" of Jesus' death will become also the "hour" of glory. In Johannine terms, the cross exalts Jesus to the fullness of glory (12:23–33), and the resurrection allows the followers of Jesus to participate in its peace

---

[279] Brown, *John*, 748–50. Cf. also J. H. Bernard, *The Gospel According to John* (Edinburgh: T & T Clark, 1928), 559.

[280] Barrett, *Gospel*, 499; Dodd, *Interpretation*, 417–418.

[281] Beasley-Murray, *John*, 295–6; Schnackenburg, *John*, 168–169; Schneider, *Johannes*, 278–291.

[282] E. Malatesta, "The literary Structure of John 17," *Biblica* 52 (1971): 190–214. Menken, *Literary Techniques*, 238–260, explores this hypothesis in further depth.

[283] Schnackenburg, *John*, 167. Cf. also C. K. Barrett's response to D. M. Smith regarding "Theories of Displacement and Redaction," *Gospel*, 21–26.

(20:19–21). The prayer of chapter 17 announces that the setting is ready for these things to take place.

This lengthy review of the research into the literary movements of John 13–17 indicates that the division suggested for the chiastic reading developed in this thesis do conform to "natural breaks" as required by Blomberg's seventh criterion. Thus, once again, there is additional reason to read the Johannine farewell discourse chiastically.

CRITERION #8: A CHIASTIC CENTER OF SIGNIFICANCE

Blomberg's eighth criterion calls for the center of the presumed macro-chiasm to be a passage worthy of that position. By this Blomberg means that the center section should have theological or ethical significance which serves to focus or summarize the major theme or themes of the chiasm as a whole. Further, according to Blomberg, the chiasm would have additional strength if the central theme or focus was clearly linked to the first and last sections of the passage as a whole. The demands of this criterion are met when 15:1–17 is understood as the chiastic center and pivot of chapters 13–17.

These verses constitute what is perhaps the most enigmatic part of the Johannine farewell discourse, Jesus' teaching about the vine and branches at the opening of chapter 15. There is inconclusive speculation about its literary genre,[284] as well as its interdependence with Old Testament[285] or rabbinic literature, or other ancient Near East

---

[284] Most commonly suggested are "allegory" (Bernard, *Good Wine*, 477; Hendriksen, *Exposition*, 293; Morris, *Gospel of John*, 668; Sloyan, *John*, 188; Tasker, *John*, 173), "parable" (Brodie, *Gospel*, 475; Calvin, *Commentary*, 107; White, *Night*, 83), "*mashal*" (Beasley-Murray, *John*, 269; Brown, *John*, 668; Mlakuzhyil, *Christocentric*, 223; Schnackenburg, *John*, 108), and "metaphor" (Segovia, *Farewell*, 134). Westcott (*Gospel*, 197) calls it a "symbolic teaching," stimulated, in part, by the procession of the company through the countryside toward the Mount of Olives. Bultmann categorically rules out "comparison" or "allegory" (*John*, 529) because of "the absence of any particle of comparison, the definite article, and the term ἀληθ[ινός]..." (ibid., n. 4). Brown (*John*, 668) believes that Bultmann properly denied Greek categories of classification, but failed to take into account the antecedents in Hebrew storytelling.

[285] E.g., Psalm 80:8ff.; Isaiah 5:1–7, 27:2–6; Jeremiah 6:9; Ezekiel 15:1–6, 17:5–10, 19:10–14; Hosea 10:1, 14:7. Cf. Dodd, *Interpretation*, 411, for a discussion relating to Psalm 80, and Bruce Vawter, "Ezekiel and John," *Catholic Biblical Quarterly* 26 (1964): 450–458, for comparisons with Ezekiel.

literary traditions.[286]   None of these investigations has proved
particularly fruitful.

A number of interpretations have been given of the role of the
vine and branches teaching in the discourse.   Three of the most
prominent approaches are those which view the teaching as a later
appendage to earlier discourse material, those which see it as a new
development which moves the meaning of the discourse in a form of
psychological stair-like ascendance, and those which understand this
section as providing the climax at the center of chiastic development.

The first approach, based on a diachronic perspective, sees a
second farewell discourse appended to the first at 15:1. The initial
discourse ended at 14:31, and now a parallel expression of it,
arising from another source within the larger Christian tradition[287]
or even perhaps another reflection on the event by the evangelist
himself,[288] moves again through many of the same themes, while
holding a slightly different focus or emphasis. There is continuity in
the sense that the same Jesus is speaking, says Schnackenburg, and
his audience remains unchanged.   However now his "gaze goes
beyond the period of separation directly to the future existence of
the disciples in the community."[289]

Painter also takes this approach, tracing the change in tone
following 15:1 to some alteration of the sociological conditions
affecting the Johannine Christian community.[290] The earliest form of
the discourse (13:31–14:31) addressed the sorrow and loss of the
disciples soon after Jesus' departure.[291] This second version (15:1–
16:4a) was added some years later when the small group of Jesus'
followers[292] had grown into a fairly significant segment of the Jewish
synagogue in their community. At that time a bitter struggle broke out
between those who considered Jesus to be the Messiah and those who
did not. Eventually the Johannine group was expelled from the
synagogue, and the discourse was modified to include a recollection of

---

[286] Following E. Schweizer (Εγω Ειμι, Göttingen: Vandenhoeck, 1939),
Bultmann (*John*, 530–531, esp. n. 5) believes the antecedents are found in the
Mandaean myth of the tree of life. Schnackenburg (*John*, 105) disagrees entirely.

[287] So Schnackenburg, *John*, 90.

[288] Painter, *Quest*, 417.

[289] Schnackenburg, *John*, 90.

[290] Painter, *Quest*, 417–35.

[291] Ibid., 423–425.

[292] Painter (*Quest*, 425) calls it the "Johannine school" and says that this
group became the nucleus of the later "Johannine community."

Jesus' own words of prophecy regarding such persecution, coupled with terms of comfort related to the presence of the παράκλητος ("Advocate").[293] Later, according to Painter, a third edition of the discourse would be appended (16:4b–16:33), this occurring after the crisis with the synagogue community had dissipated.[294] Left to its isolation within the Greco-Roman world this Johannine community of faith is in danger of turning in on itself. In this context there is a need for the reassurance of Jesus' imminent return (16:16), and the sustaining ministry of the unifying παράκλητος ("Advocate") (16:5–15).

A similar perspective is widely held among exegetes,[295] though most find more commonality throughout the sections of chapters 15 and 16, and thus keep them together as a larger literary unit. Though there is an affinity with the themes of 13:31–14:31, the substance of this second rendition of the discourse material either came from another hand, or displays a reworking of the ideas of the first textual expression of it, but at a different historical moment when the need of the community had changed.[296]

Representing the second perspective, Barrett sees the vine and branches discourse as a meditation on the themes of the Jewish Feast of Tabernacles,[297] which, he believes, would be prominent in the minds of the disciples because of the allusions in the Passover celebration to the travels of Israel in the wilderness. The "meditation" is located at this point in the farewell discourse as a unit because it follows logically on the premonitions of the passion which end chapter 14. If the disciples (or members of the larger faith community) are to benefit

---

[293] Ibid., 425–428. See also J. Louis Martyn, *The Gospel of John in Christian History* (New York: Paulist Press, 1979) as well as his *History & Theology*. Also C. K. Barrett, *The Gospel According to St John* (London: SPCK, 1978), 361–362.

[294] Painter, *Quest*, 428–432.

[295] Cf. Blank, *Gospel*, 14–15; Brown, *John*, 588; Beasley-Murray, *John*, 269; Brodie, *Gospel*, 429–430; Deeks, "Structure," 119–120; Pryor, *John*, 102–103.

[296] Hendriksen (*Exposition*, 291) does not support the general "dislocation" or "multiple stages" development of the farewell discourse as a whole. However, he is willing to admit "the possibility of *topical* (instead of strictly *chronological*) arrangement" for various pericopes in the discourse. For instance, the vine and branches teaching "may have been spoken a little earlier, in connection with the institution of the Lord's Supper (the drinking of the 'fruit of the vine')." It was recorded in its present location because, from the perspective of topical development, it seems to fit better as it now stands.

[297] Barrett, *Gospel According to St John*, 470–471.

from Jesus' death, they must be bound to him in a union that needs to be described in graphic terms such as these metaphors. Hence the discourse continues to build in intensity, placing the followers of Jesus who may despair at his leaving (chapter 14) in a vital psychological and spiritual link with him (15:1–17).

Lightfoot is even more explicit regarding the development that takes place at this point. "St. John seems to wish his readers to perceive that the revelation becomes clearer and deeper, as we go forward by degrees towards the passion."[298] To put it more concretely, "in spite of the last words of 14:31, there is to be no change of scene at present, the advance in the instruction and the advance in the action are shown to be parallel throughout."[299] Others, such as Dodd,[300] hold a similar view. There is a new stage in the teaching of the farewell discourse at 15:1, but it rises from the call of 14:31. Rather than a command to move physically, this exhortation functions as a more intense urging for the listener to exercise the kind of spiritual discipline that will allow himself or herself to be elevated symbolically and supernaturally into the glory of the Son of the Father.

Bultmann[301] and Bernard[302] also see new insights being developed at this point in the farewell discourse. Bultmann identifies the vine and branches teaching as a "commentary on 13:34f"[303] at minimum, and possibly on the larger expanse of the footwashing episode in 13:1–20 as well. Bernard takes the view, similar to Barrett's, that there is a Eucharistic homily behind this teaching, and wishes to relocate it immediately following the last supper which was briefly introduced by the opening scene of 13:1–31.

Another sacramental approach is put forward by Westcott.[304] In his desire to maintain the integrity of the full discourse as it now stands, and, at the same time, to be faithful to the leave-taking of 14:31, he suggests that these words were spoken while Jesus and his disciples meandered toward the Garden of Gethsemane. That trek would place them either in the vicinity of the vineyards of the Kidron

---

[298] Lightfoot, *St. John's Gospel*, 277.

[299] Ibid., 277–278.

[300] Dodd, *Interpretation*, 416. Cf. also Calvin, *Commentary*, 106; Morris, *John*, 661; Newbigin, *The Light Has Come* (Grand Rapids: Eerdmans, 1982), 193–194; Tasker, *Gospel*, 170.

[301] Bultmann, *John*, 529–530.

[302] Bernard, *Good Wine*, 476–477.

[303] Bultmann, *John*, 529.

[304] Westcott, *Gospel*, 196–197.

valley or near the images of golden vines surrounding the gates of the Temple as Jesus spoke these words. Thus there would be continuity with the earlier teachings of Jesus as the farewell discourse progressed, but now the altered environment would offer Jesus a unique opportunity to give an object lesson that would build upon his previous exhortations.

The third major interpretation of the vine and branches teaching identifies the first part of John 15 as the chiastic center of the entire discourse. Since chiastically shaped literary units are built with sections of *inclusio* balanced in parallel on either side of a key central passage, the "heart" of meaning for the passage as a whole belongs to that interior element. Some have found the opening verses of John 15 to function in that manner within the farewell discourse.

For Ellis, 15:1–25 constitutes the chiastic center. This is the heart of the discourse, according to Ellis, and, in fact, contains the promise that holds the other passages together in some coherent unity. Jesus' departure from the disciples will create a "gap" in which persecution and internal doubting might rob them of both faith and fruitfulness. Only if they remain connected spiritually to Jesus will they have the resources to both increase the strength of their faith and cause it to blossom with deeds that reflect their relationship with Jesus.[305]

More consonant with traditional divisions of the Johannine farewell discourse is Mlakuzhyil's approach.[306] His reading of chapters 13–17 includes six sub-units: C (13:1–13:38+[307]), D (13:31–14:31), E (15:1–15:17), E[1] (15:18–16:4d), D[1] (16:4e–16:33), and C[1] (17:1–17:26).[308] Although Mlakuzhyil recognises the integrity of

---

[305] Barnhart, *Good Wine*, builds his elaborate "chiastic mandala" on Ellis' structures in a "spatial" reading of the gospel. Although his approach expands upon Ellis' work in broadening the dimensions of balance and symmetry, it does little to add to his perceived units of structure.

[306] Mlakuzhyil, *Christocentric*, 223–225.

[307] Mlakuzhyil (*Christocentric*, 223) identifies 13:31–38 as "bridge verses" which have an intricate connection to both sections C and D, and therefore are included in the verses represented by both sections.

[308] C (13,1–38+):   The symbolic act of the hour (feet-washing) and the prediction of betrayal and denial.

D (13,31–14,31):   The prediction of Peter's denials and the first farewell discourse.

E (15:1–17):   The allegory of the vine and the branches and the commandment of love.

15:1–17 as a literary unit,[309] he pairs these verses with the next section (15:18–16:4d) so that they together forming the chiastic center of the discourse.

When 15:1–17 is read as the chiastic center of the farewell discourse a number of exegetical issues are resolved in a meaningful way. First, the unique character of the vine and branches teaching makes sense as it pertains to the whole of the discourse. Rather than intruding as a strange form of teaching, out of place in the rest of the running monologue, it now becomes the climax around which the rest of the discourse turns. Everything that Jesus says and does among the disciples in this farewell discourse is intended to draw them into a deep and abiding relationship with himself. Insofar as that relationship develops, the blessings he announces will unfold (peace in a troubled world; spiritual clarity and strength; union with the Father; confidence in times of crisis; expressions of loving behaviour). Whenever that relationship is severed or diminished, the reverse of these blessings results, to the point of betrayal and separation from the Father.

Second, the problem of the dangling command to arise and leave in 14:31b may be put into perspective. The argument that it belongs at this point because it announces the call to a higher plateau of spirituality does not have support in the tone or content of the rest of the dialogue. The best explanation for its present location is that it was found originally at the close of one of the earlier farewell discourse traditions that was incorporated into this newer version of the discourse by a redactor. The redactor's intent, however, was not to rewrite all of the elements of the traditions so that they would give birth to a different, seamless account of the discourse. Rather, the various farewell discourse materials were joined in such a way that they created a new arrangement of the teachings of Jesus which now brought a new focus to the discussion, that of Jesus' instruction to "abide in me." The dangling command of 14:31b becomes, in this reading, a marker indicating the end of the first half of the discourse,

---

E[1] (15,18–16,4d):   The hatred and persecution by the
                       world, and the disciple's witnessing.

D[1] (16,4e–33):   The second farewell discourse
                    and the prediction of the disciple's desertion.

C[1] (17,1–26):   The prayer of the hour [of Jesus' passion-
                   death-resurrection].

[309] Mlakuzhyil, *Christocentric*, 224.

along with a call to recognise the teaching that follows it as the apex of the chiastic movement.

Third, in this reading the "love command" of 15:12–17 provides a link to both the gathering scene and the departing prayer. Each of those sections ends with what appears to be a later redactional insertion of an echo of the love command.

Understood in this manner the vine and branches teaching of 15:1–17 stands alone in the discourse, with no clear mirroring in any of the other sections. Moreover, through the central thrust of the vine and branches teaching, Jesus' exhortation for the disciples to "abide in me," forms a challenge which serve as the cohesive glue that summarises the meaning of the discourse and binds together its multiple sections:

- The washing episode (A) and prayer (A$_1$) are designed to bring the disciples into a unique relationship with Jesus and the Father.
- In B and B$_1$ the disciples are warned of the heartbreak of desertion which separates them from the special relationship Jesus wishes them to have with himself.
- Jesus' exhortations in C and C$_1$ temper the unrest that was caused in the disciples' hearts by the announcement of Jesus' imminent departure. Here Jesus gives a promise that the relationship between them and himself will be strengthened even in Jesus' physical absence. The means to this strengthening will be an exercise of the Father's spiritual power.
- In sections D and D$_1$ the mode of spiritual union that allows the disciples to abide in Jesus is described as a unique dispensation of the παράκλητος ("Advocate").
- The troubles which the disciples' unique relationship with Jesus will cause are identified in sections E and E$_1$.

Most prominently, the vine and branches teaching carries with it a resounding exhortation for the disciples to "abide in" Jesus. This theme pervades the discourse as a whole, and reaches its apex in the explicit references of John 15:1–17. Thus Blomberg's eighth criterion for assessing macro-chiasm is met in this reading of the Johannine farewell discourse.

Moreover, the chiastic outline presented here is consistent, with no "ruptures" or unusual shifts that step out of the typical chiastic sequence. Because of the consistency of the chiastic development in this reading of John 13–17 Blomberg's final criterion is also met.

Summary

In establishing his criteria for assessing macro-chiasm Blomberg acknowledges that "these nine criteria are seldom fulfilled *in toto* even by well-established chiastic structures."[310]   He indicates that any "hypothesis which fulfills most of all of the nine stands a strong chance of reflecting the actual structure of the text in question."[311]   Since the chiastic reading of John 13–17 offered above meets all nine of Blomberg's criteria there is strong affirmation for viewing the development of the Johannine farewell discourse in this manner.

Since other chiastic approaches have been offered for these chapters, it is important to test them as well by Blomberg's nine criteria. To this we turn next.

---

[310] Blomberg, "Structure," 7.
[311] Ibid.

CHAPTER 8

OTHER CHIASTIC APPROACHES

Finding the Best Chiastic Development

As noted throughout this discussion, there are others who have similarly suggested that John 13–17 is an expression of macro–chiasm. In order to further affirm the validity of the reading offered here it is important to compare this reading with similar chiastic approaches.

Ellis

For Ellis, who sees the entire Fourth Gospel as developed chiastically, chapters 13–17 constitute "Sequence 18" of the whole.[1] Five "sections" make up this "sequence":

A	The gathering scene		13:1–32
	B	The first discourse	13:33–14:31
		C The vine and branches teaching	15:1–25
	B¹	The second discourse	15:26–16:33
A¹	The prayer		17:1–26

---

[1] Ellis, *Genius*, 14–5, 210–211. Howard-Brook (*Becoming Children of God*, 289–290) also follows Ellis' chiastic outline of chapters 13–17.

The heart of the discourse, section C, is the high point of Jesus' teaching in chapters 13–17, according to Ellis, and, in fact, contains the promise that holds the other passages together in some coherent unity. Jesus' departure from the disciples will create a "gap" in which outside persecution and internal doubting might possibly rob them of both faith and fruitfulness. Only if they remain connected spiritually to Jesus will they have the resources to both increase the strength of their faith and cause it to blossom with deeds that reflect their relationship with Jesus.

Ellis' work often presses hard at the edges of credibility. In his search for chiasm, almost all other exegetical conventions are ignored at one time or another,[2] violating Blomberg's seventh criterion. In his analysis of chapter 13, for instance, Ellis needs to include verses 31–32 with the introductory section, creating a break in the literary flow after verse 32. This is necessary in order to have the references to the glorification of the Son of Man in these verses fall into a section that will parallel the final section of the discourse, chapter 17, where similar references to a glorification of the Son of Man occur. Since, at the same time, the bulk of references to Jesus' leaving happen in chapter 16, and not in chapter 17, Ellis needs the expressions of 13:33–38 to fall into the second section of his outline of the discourse. In this view he is virtually alone. Furthermore, Ellis' chiastic outline identifies only five sections over the full length of the farewell discourse, with the second (13:33–14:31) and fourth (15:26–16:33) segments containing so much material that the parallels between the two are far from clear and distinct. In this Ellis fails to conform to Blomberg's criteria three, four and six. It is obvious that the chiastic developments Ellis outlines are not convincing.

Simoens

A far more insightful chiastic reading of the Johannine farewell discourse is that put forward by Simoens.[3] He summarises the approaches taken by eight Johannine scholars[4] in their attempts to sort,

---

[2] Cf. Ashton, *Studying John*, 141–165.

[3] Simoens, *La Gloire d'aimer*.

[4] Ibid., 1–51: A. Loisy, A. Durand, M.-J. Lagrange, Gächter, R. Bultmann, C. H. Dodd, R. E. Brown, B. Lindars, R. Schnackenburg, M.-E. Boismard/A. Lamouille.

arrange, or outline the materials of John 13–17. He is very appreciative of Brown's mediating work between the strongly diverging opinions of Bultmann and Dodd.[5] More than that, he finds great merit in what, for Brown, was a tentative suggestion of a possible chiastic development in the materials of the farewell discourse.[6]

Simoens' survey of the field of interpretations of the Johannine farewell discourse results in the conclusion that, for the most part, most other scholars have fallen under the "allure" of diachronic redactionary readings.[7] His approach, in contrast, focuses on the literary design of the received text as a "coherent ensemble."[8] His examination is carried out within the context of his own structural analysis rooted in the historic investigation of the discipline.[9]

Simoens' structural analysis relies heavily on perceived patterns of repetition that form *inclusio* at all levels of textual development. In fact, as the smaller elements of *inclusio* begin to emerge, they are quickly drawn up into more comprehensive systems of concentric symmetry and parallelism. In the end Simoens argues for a seven-part development to the farewell discourse, $ABCDC^1B^1A^1$, with the first half repeated thematically (albeit sometimes inverted in order) in the second half, and the entire movement balancing on either side of the "love command" of 15:12–17. It is, in Simoens' estimate, a beautifully articulated geometrically shaped whole,[10] and is diagrammed in the following manner:

---

[5] Simoens, *La Gloire d'aimer*, 26.

[6] Ibid., 28ff., reflecting on Brown, *John*, 597.

[7] Simoens, *La Gloire d'aimer*, 51: "La majorité des études sur ces chapitres, depuis le XIXe siècle, sont d'allure diachronique."

[8] Ibid.: "La tâche s'impose donc de porter un regard impartial à la fois sur la forme littéraire et sur le contenu théologique, pour toutes les parties du texte, en considérant Jn 13 – 17 comme un ensemble cohérent dans son état définitif et comme une pièce maîtresse du quatrième évangile, déterminante pour son interprétation."

[9] Ibid., 54–55.

[10] Ibid., 67: "Sous forme de figure géométrique..." It is this visual balance that leads some to question whether the form is imposed for effect rather than inherent in the literary development of the text itself. Cf. Joseph Cahill's review in *Catholic Biblical Quarterly* 45 (1983): 709–711.

A   *Agapè*/Glorification[11]   13:1–38

    B   Encouragement/*Agapè*-garde de la parole/Départ 14:1–31

        C   Demeurer/Joie   15:1–11

            D   *Agapè* mutuelle   15:12–17

        C_1 Haine du monde/Persécution-Exclusion par
                           ignorance   15:18–16:3

    B_1 Départ/Joie/Encouragement   16:4–33

A_1 Glorification/*Agapè*   17:1–26

While the parallel sections of this chiastic movement contain the same basic themes, Simoens notes that the reflexive units reverse the multiple ideas he finds in each. More specifically, Simoens' outermost subunits (13:1–38; 17:1–26) explore the themes of love and glorification. However, since the initial section moves by way of love to the glorification of Jesus among his disciples, and the latter anticipates Jesus' ultimate glorification through the loving act of the Father, the order of these themes is reversed the one from the other. 13:1–38 opens the scene that will bring glory by speaking of love; the prayer of chapter 17 highlights the coming glory as a product of the love of the Father through the Son to the disciples and their kin, and ends on that note of love.

Further, the middle components of Simoens' arrangement (14:1–31; 16:4–33) deal with the themes of Jesus' impending departure and the encouragement the disciples will receive by way of the παράκλητος ("Advocate"). Again, the order of treatment is somewhat inverted, with chapter 14 speaking about Jesus' departure more at the end and 16 near the beginning, and the location of encouragement at the other position in each chapter.

Third, the innermost subunits (15:1–11; 15:18–16:3) address pairs of themes: joy/hatred and abiding/persecution-exclusion. As before, the order in the second section reverses the order in the first.

---

[11] The mixture of languages (French, English and Greek) in Simoens' outline is his own choice.

Simoens is thus able to identify a non-parallel "center" (15:12–17) which summarises the entire discourse with the love command, which both harks back to the opening and anticipates the closing of the whole.

Simoens takes his analysis one step further in terms of the functional nature of chapter 17. He has already identified internal elements of *inclusio* and repetition within each section. Now he finds additional analogous interaction between segments of the prayer and sections of the discourse. For instance, 17:1–5 reflects the emphasis in chapter 13 on the glorification of the Son by the Father. 17:6–11 mirrors themes of "keeping" and "being kept" which are otherwise expressed in chapter 14. 17:12–13 speaks of the joy that is received through faithful obedience, a theme that is similarly described in the vine and branches teaching of 15:1–11. In 17:14a Jesus says ἐγὼ δέδωκα αὐτοῖς τὸν λόγον σου,[12] which Simoens reads as an echo of Jesus' giving the new command in 15:12–17. 17:14b–19 calls for the guarding of the disciples as they endure the struggles thrust upon them by this hostile world, a theme Jesus spoke about earlier in 15:18–16:3. In 17:20–23 Jesus expresses his desire for his disciples to enter into his glory, and that this transformation will be fully accomplished only upon his departure from them; similar themes unfold in 16:4–33. Finally, Simoens sees the concluding verses of chapter 17 as the symbolic essence of the entire prayer, and suggests that they reflect back upon the whole of the chapter as a miniature distillation of the entirety. In this way Simoens adds another layer of stratification to the parallelism he already deduced in the chiasm of the passage. Unfortunately, as the complexity of his interweavings increases, the clarity decreases, as does the likelihood that all of these levels of meaning were able to function overtly for the evangelist or redactor, or reader, for that matter.

As Simoens develops these analogies, parallels, and multiple instances of *inclusio*, his understanding of the literary structure of the farewell discourse becomes more and more complicated. This is precisely the criticism levelled by his detractors. Cahill wonders, for instance, whether Simoens limits himself to analyses of literary design based almost exclusively on a search for incidences of parallelism and *inclusio*, and thus forces a chiastic reading of the passage.[13] Further,

---

[12] "I have given them your word…"

[13] Joseph Cahill, review, *Catholic Biblical Quarterly,* 45 (1983): 709–11, 710. See also the review by A. Lamouille in *Revue Biblique,* 89: 627–629.

he says, "this visual symmetry never quite imposes itself into an intellectual control of the literature itself."[14] Likewise Brodie, who admires the creative genius of Simoens' proposals, does not agree that they are rooted in the movement of the text itself, and prefers instead to view the development of the farewell discourse as a progressive linear movement that builds in energy toward the prayer of chapter 17.[15]

In a manner similar to that of Ellis, Simoens perceives a great deal of parallel repetition of words and themes in the farewell discourse across a chiastic center. However, an additional factor that shapes Simoens' selection of literary segments in the discourse is his contention that John 13–17 functions as a "covenant" document.[16] Reflecting on Brown's suggestion that there are a number of similarities between Moses' farewell discourse in Deuteronomy and that of Jesus,[17] Simoens advances the idea that the genre of both Deuteronomy and John 13–17 surpasses that of mere farewell discourse and ought, instead, to be considered the language of covenant documents. Using L'Hour's research on the structure of covenant documents,[18] Simoens outlines five sections having similar character in both texts:[19]

1. Historical Prologue (Deuteronomy 1:1–4:40; John 13).
2. Great Commandment (Deuteronomy 4:44–11:32; John 14).
3. Stipulations (Deuteronomy 12:1–26:15; John 15:1–16:3).
4. Blessings and Curses (Deuteronomy 26:16–30:20; John 16:4–33).
5. Summary Hymn (Deuteronomy 32–33; John 17).

The outcome of this double layer of literary intent means, of course, that Simoens must be sure that his chiastic structures and these covenant document units coincide. As a result, Simoens requires that the two inner literary sub-units (15:1–11; 15:18–

---

[14] Ibid.

[15] Thomas L. Brodie, *The Gospel according to John: a Literary and Theological Commentary* (New York: Oxford University Press, 1993), 429.

[16] Simoens, *La Gloire d'aimer*, 202–203.

[17] Brown, *Gospel*, 600: Moses chooses Joshua as successor, Jesus promises Paraclete as successor; Moses calls down God's blessing on Israel, Jesus concludes with a call for the Father's blessing on the new people of God.

[18] J. L'Hour, *La Morale de l'alliance,* Cahiers de la Revue Biblique 5 Paris 1966.

[19] Simoens, *La Gloire d'aimer*, 204.

16:3) and the center around which the whole chiastic structure is designed (15:12–17) all be located in the central section of the arrangement required by matrix of covenant documents. In this manner Simoens' insights become the slave of his own system. As Segovia notes, the overall chiastic structure grows more and more complex, until it looks very good when diagrammed on paper, but does not lend itself to easy apprehension in a simple reading of the text.[20] Further, as the two systems are cross-referenced, chiastic parallelism and covenant document sections do not entirely correspond, and Simoens fails to define his literary segments according to the natural breaks suggested by the text, one of the minimal requirements for macro-chiasm identified in Blomberg's seventh criterion. Furthermore, the multiple themes found in Simoens' segments B (14:1–31) and B₁ (16:4–33) do not provide the clarity of parallelism demanded by Blomberg's fifth and sixth criteria. Nor does the chiastic center identified by Simoens, 15:12–17, express what Blomberg's eighth criterion would see as a heightened or significant climax to the discourse as a whole when separated from 15:1–11. Besides, says Segovia, Simoens has not given substantive proof that John 13–17 functions as a covenant document either within the Fourth Gospel or on its own, nor does he explain how his synchronic reading of the discourse answers the diachronic problems that continue to show themselves as conundrums in the text.

Mlakuzhyil

Similar issues detract from the proposal of Mlakuzhyil. While he examines with profit particular pericopes in the Fourth Gospel, finding much that may be read chiastically, he also goes further and develops an analysis of the gospel as a whole that is pressed into that particular literary arrangement. The result is another delightful set of diagrams, geometrically balanced, charting the contents of the entire gospel from end to end. Yet, at the same time, these parallel units are couched in an extremely intricate framework, so complex as to prevent the structure from becoming useful either as a literary device to guide the initial designs of writing or editing, or again as a fruitful

---

[20] Segovia, *Farewell*, 40.

communications tool for clearly expressing a central message or a balanced pairing of emphases.

Mlakuzhyil finds chiasm after chiasm throughout the Fourth Gospel. The farewell discourse of John 13–17, while included by Mlakuzhyil within several other chiastic "arcs,"[21] also forms an integrated chiastically developed section in its own right, according to his view.

Mlakuzhyil sees the footwashing episode of chapter 13 and the prayer of chapter 17 as forming the first and last "subsections" of the discourse.[22] He acknowledges that there is significant disagreement among scholars in identifying the point at which the first subsection ends.[23] In an attempt to use the literary movements and breaks developed in several different analyses, he chooses to identify 13:31–38 as a "bridge section" belonging to both the first and the second literary subunits.[24] Therefore 13:1–38 constitutes the first full subunit of the chiasm, while 13:31–14:31 becomes the second subunit. Following Schnackenburg[25] over against Simoens,[26] who takes 15:1–16:3 as a subunit, Mlakuzhyil identifies 15:1–17 as the next and central pericope. In fact, it is "precisely on account of the *antithetical parallelism* (or contrast) between 15,1–17 and 15,18–16,4a [that] these could be considered as two literary units."[27] Further, according to Mlakuzhyil, there is both a "change of subject matter" at 15:18 that distinguishes 15:18–16:4d from the preceding section,[28] and other elements of *inclusio* and parallelism which call for 15:1–17 to be considered independent of the following verses. Still, in an effort to recognise the close connection between 15:1–17 and 15:18–16:4e, Mlakuzhyil posits that these two subunits together form the chiastic focal point of the passage.[29] Further, since "a new literary genre (prayer) begins at 17,1, it is clear that 16,33 is the end of the literary unit

---

[21] Mlakuzhyil's term for the chiastic units he finds throughout the gospel.

[22] Mlakuzhyil, *Christocentric*, 221.

[23] Ibid.

[24] Ibid., 223.

[25] Schnackenburg, *John*, 91–92.

[26] Simoens, *La Gloire d'aimer*, 130–132.

[27] Mlakuzhyil, *Christocentric*, 224.

[28] Mlakuzhyil, *Christocentric*, 224.

[29] Ibid., 225.

which begins at 16,4e."[30] The outcome of Mlakuzhyil's investigations produces a chiastic ordering of the elements of the Johannine farewell discourse in the following manner:

A   The symbolic act of the hour (the feet-washing)
      and the prediction of betrayal and denial.   13:1–38

    B   The prediction of Peter's denials
        and the first farewell discourse.   13:31–14:31

        C   The allegory of the vine and the branches
           and the commandment of love.   15:1–17

        C_1 The hatred and persecution by the world,
           and the disciples' witnessing.   15:18–16:4d

    B_1 The second farewell discourse
        and the prediction of the disciples' desertion.   16:4e–33

A_1 The prayer of the hour.   17:1–26

While this analysis pays close attention to the literary development of the text, there are at least three major difficulties. First, the "bridge" section of 13:31–38 denies chiastic simplicity and is contrary to Blomberg's seventh criterion. Either these verses belong to the previous literary subunit or they belong to the literary subunit that follows. Chiasm is understood as reflexive parallelism of literary units across the midpoint of a passage. When sections of the literary development appear to be needed in a double use to substantiate chiastic moves, the whole purpose of the chiastic development ceases to function.

Second, the literary subunits that Mlakuzhyil identifies are far too broad, for the most part, and thus not meeting the requirements set out in Blomberg's third through sixth criteria. Section C_1, for instance,

---

[30] Ibid., 226.

contains several elements that are much more closely linked to his Section B than they are with his C.[31]

Third, in violation of Blomberg's eighth criterion, Mlakuzhyil's chiastic development does not identify a clear central section that has a climactic character. Instead, Mlakuzhyil pairs together two sections[32] that have little in common with one another. While it is possible, as Thomson suggests, to have chiastic movements in which the two central elements are paired with one another in a symbiotic union that creates a centered climax, or to have the reflexive turn between halves occur as a literary break between the central sections of the chiasm, the central elements, joined in tandem as they are in Mlakuzhyil's chiasm, serve neither as a climactic pair nor function well in reflective parallelism.

Unfortunately, by the time Mlakuzhyil returns to the theological affirmations that are supposed to outline his study of the Fourth Gospel, he uses few of the strict chiastic rules of investigation he had committed himself to using in order to derive support for his "Christocentric" theses.[33] The result is that Mlakuzhyil acknowledges the reflexive parallelism of some of the repetitious elements in the farewell discourse, but he does not provide an adequate analysis of the passage that would conform to the chiastic assessment criteria of Blomberg. What is needed is an understanding of the macro-chiastic reflexive parallelism clearly present in the discourse that also pays close attention to the data of the text as explored through the tools of historical criticism.

As we have shown in Chapter Seven, when one pays careful attention to the developments of the text of the discourse, there are a number of literary segments that begin to emerge and relate to one another in the reflexive parallelism of chiasm. Ellis, and those who follow his lead,[34] have not paid close enough attention to the details of the text, and thus fail to establish chiastic outlines that sustain rigorous examination. Simoens and Mlakuzhyil began their investigations properly, observing the repetition and parallelism present throughout the Johannine farewell discourse. Both, however, were derailed by secondary issues that pressed their chiastic assessments out of focus,

---

[31] E.g., the coming of the παράκλητος ("Advocate") (14:26; 15:26); the advance teaching of Jesus that serves to protect the disciples (14:25; 16:1).

[32] C (15:1–17) and C_1 (15:18–16:4d).

[33] Mlakuzhyil, *Christocentric*, 349–351.

[34] Particularly Howard-Brook and Barnhart.

and failed to take into account more of the nuances of change and movement in the text itself.

Still, their analyses confirm the reflexive parallelism that is clearly present in the John 13–17. The chiastic outline presented in Chapter Six and investigated under the assessment criteria of Blomberg in Chapter Seven take the best interpretations of Simoens and Mlakuzhyil and bring them to a more critically secure development.

CHAPTER 9

CONCLUSIONS

John 13–17 as Macro-Chiasm

Obviously, more work needs to be done in researching chiasm in the literature of antiquity. It is clear at this stage of chiastic investigations, however, that the literary tool of micro-chiasm was used widely by the authors of both the Hebrew Bible and the New Testament. There is also ample evidence of macro-chiasm in longer sections of these collections. What remains somewhat unclear is the specific relationship between micro-chiasm and macro-chiasm. While micro-chiasm appears to have developed as an extended form of poetic parallelism, its reflexive movements of thought seem to have taken on expanded form in longer narratives that show less precision with verbal parallels yet, at the same time, having similar mirroring characteristics between sections having paralleled themes and structures.

The chiastic reading of John 13–17 presented in this study results in an interpretation of the farewell discourse that addresses a number of important issues in Fourth Gospel studies. It offers, for instance, an intelligible role for the repeated "love command," showing it to be part of the chiastic framing and centering of the discourse as a whole. Furthermore, it highlights the significance of the vine and branches teaching in 15:1–17, allowing it to stand prominently as the turning point around which the discourse is built, and using its metaphor as the guiding principle by which the rest of the teachings of the discourse hold together.[1] Finally, it balances the introductory narrative, shaped by its expression of union with Jesus at entrance into the hour of glory, with the concluding prayer, where, once again union with Jesus is shown to take place in the experience of the hour of glory.[2]

Indeed, this approach has potential for bringing together some of the best understandings developed by the otherwise divergent synchronic and diachronic readings of John 13–17. Each of those readings is based on a linear movement of either the text or some perceived psychological development behind the text. The synchronic readings too quickly dismiss the disjunctures of the passage at its literary level as if these do not much matter. The diachronic readings, on the other hand, cannot seem to find a comprehensive understanding of the text as its stands, focusing instead upon the meaning of portions of the discourse and their presumed history.

If, however, the sections of the discourse as they have been collected and edited in the final redaction hold together in a chiastic reading, the disjunctions take on new significance. The strange ending of chapter 14 can be recognised as both a lingering indication of redactive editing as well as a signal announcing the move from one section to the next, perhaps even hinting at some of the multiple levels of meaning Brodie suggested, particularly with reference to the crowning apex of chiastic design that follows in the vine and branches teaching of 15:1–17. The repetitious elements of the discourse begin to make sense as parallel teachings on common themes. The character of the vine and branches teaching becomes more obvious, in its role as the chiastic pivot, shaping the flow of meaning for the discourse as a whole. Jesus' ministry is one that incorporates the disciples into the glory he shares with the father. He creates the context in which they will abide in him (13:1–35; 17:1–26), producing a community of mutual love. If they should fail to

---

[1] Spiritual attachment to Jesus brings one into the circle of divine glory (13:1–30; 17:1–26), safeguards against the tendencies toward denial (13:36–38; 16:29–33), creates a context in which Jesus' departure holds comfort (14:1–14; 16:16–28), is given substance by way of the Spirit (14:15–26; 16:4b–15), and provides endurance in the face of persecution by the world (14:27–31; 15:18–16:4a).

[2] Note that in each instance Judas is removed at the time of the cleansing motif, and is separated from the subsequent glory: 13:18, 17:12.

abide in him, life becomes very dark (13:36–38; 16:29–33). In view of Jesus' imminent departure, therefore, abiding in Jesus takes on eschatological overtones (14:1–14; 16:16–28). The παράκλητος ("Advocate") becomes the spiritual link by which the disciples are able to abide in a physically absent Jesus (14:15–26; 16:4b–15), and threats to disrupting this linkage create a challenging context for living faithfully (14:27–31; 15:18–16:4a).

This chiastic reading of the discourse goes beyond previous approaches to John 13–17 in several ways. First, it shows the significance of the central teaching of the vine and branches as the focus of the passage rather than just a thematic turn along the way. In the other readings of the discourse emphasis is often placed upon the meal (e.g., Brown, Schnackenburg) or on the discourse as a farewell (e.g., Segovia, Brodie), or even upon the history of the community in which the discourse is transmitted (e.g., Painter).

Second the prominent sections that begin (the outward union of the disciples with Jesus through the washing of the footwashing scene) and end (the inner union of the disciples with Jesus through the sanctification offered in his prayer) the discourse are understood as parallel explications of the central theme: "Abide in me!" The discourse holds together, in this reading, and the footwashing scene is directly linked to the theology of the passage. Similarly, the prayer in chapter 17 is neither the climax nor the summary of the discourses. Instead, it functions to conclude the discourses as a sort of reflection to the footwashing scene, confirming the intimate connection between Jesus and his disciples.

Third, the otherwise cumbersome repetition of themes, from the small references focusing on denial, to the larger investigations of the work of the Spirit, would be understood, in this reading, as a means by which the flow of the discourse in its entirety would be shepherded along a meaningful movement ascending and descending paired stairs, bringing the reader up toward or down from the central thrust of the whole.

In this manner a chiastic reading of the Johannine farewell discourse provides new insight. If the text of the Fourth Gospel as it has come to us, with the farewell discourse developed in its present formation, is a finished product designed to convey meaning and significance related to the person and teachings of Jesus, the chiastic reading of John 13–17 presented here offers an interpretive approach that can provide a new way in which to bring together the insights provided by both the diachronic and synchronic readings of the text. Moreover, it encourages recognition that the multiple sections of the farewell discourse reflect each other and build upon one another in a manner that allows the whole to become more than the sum of its parts.

BIBLIOGRAPHY

Achtemeier, Paul J. and Elizabeth. *The Old Testament Roots of Our Faith*. Philadelphia: Fortress, 1962.

Agourides, S. C. "The 'High-Priestly Prayer' of Jesus," *Studia Evangelica* 4 (1968): 137–143.

Allen, Leslie C. *Psalms 101–150*. Word Biblical Commentary 21. Waco: Word, 1983.

Alonso Schökel, L. *Estudios de poética hebrea*. Barcelona: Flors, 1963.

Alden, R. L. "Chiastic Psalms: A Study in the Mechanics of Semitic Poetry in Psalms 1–50," *Journal of the Evangelical Theological Society* 17 (1974): 11–28.

Alter, Robert. *The Art of Biblical Poetry*. New York: Harper Basic Books, 1985.

————. *The Art of Biblical Narrative*. New York: Basic Books, 1992.

————. *The World of Biblical Literature*. New York: Basic Books, 1992.

Anderson, B. W. "From Analysis to Synthesis: The Interpretation of Gen 1–11," *Journal of Biblical Literature* 97 (1978): 23–39.

Ashton, John, Ed. *The Interpretation of John*. Philadelphia: Fortress, 1986.

————. *Understanding the Fourth Gospel*. Oxford: Clarendon Press, 1991.

————. *Studying John*. Oxford: Clarendon Press, 1994.

Augustine. "Lectures on the Gospel according to St. John," *Nicene and Post-Nicene Fathers*, 1st ser., vol. 7. Grand Rapids: Eerdmans, 1978: 1–452.

Aune, David E. *The New Testament in Its Literary Environment*. Philadelphia: Westminster, 1987.

Bailey, Kenneth E. *Poet and Peasant: A Literary-Cultural Approach to the Parables in Luke*. Grand Rapids: Eerdmans, 1976.

————. *Through Peasant Eyes: More Lucan Parables*. Grand Rapids: Eerdmans, 1980.

Baker, David L. *Two Testaments, One Bible: A Study of the Theological Relationship between the Old & New Testaments*, rev. ed. Downers Grove, Illinois: InterVarsity Press, 1991.

Baldwin, Joyce. *Haggai, Zechariah, Malachi.* Tyndale Old Testament Commentaries. Downers Grove: InterVarsity Press, 1972.

Barnhart, Bruno. *The Good Wine: Reading from the Center.* New York: Paulist Press, 1993.

Barrett, C. K. *Essays on John.* London: SPCK, 1982.

————. *The Gospel According to St John.* London: SPCK, 1978.

————. *The Gospel of John and Judaism.* London: SPCK, 1975.

Barth, Markus. *Ephesians 1–3.* Anchor Bible 34. Garden City, New York: Doubleday and Company, 1974.

Barthes, Roland, et al. *Structural Analysis and Biblical Exegesis.* Pittsburgh Theological Monograph Series 3. Pittsburgh: Pickwick, 1974.

Beasley-Murray, George. *John.* Word Biblical Commentary 36. Waco, Texas: Word, 1987.

Bernard, J. H. *The Gospel According to St. John.* International Critical Commentary. Edinburgh: T & T Clark, 1928.

Bertman, Stephen. "Symmetrical Design in the Book of Ruth," *Journal of Biblical Literature* 84 (1965): 165–168.

Blank, Josef. *The Gospel According to St. John,* Vol. 2. New York: Crossroad, 1981.

Bliese, Loren F. "Chiastic and Homogeneous Metrical Structures Enhanced by Word Patterns in Obadiah," *Journal of Translation and Text Linguistics* 6 (1993): 210–227.

Bligh, John. *Galatians in Greek, A Structural Analysis of St. Paul's Epistle to the Galatians.* Detroit: University of Detroit Press, 1966.

Blomberg, Craig. "The Structure of 2 Corinthians 1–7," *Criswell Theological Review* 4 (1989): 3–20.

Boling, Robert G. *Judges.* Anchor Bible 6A. Garden City, New York: Doubleday, 1975.

Borgen, Peder. *Philo, John and Paul: New Perspectives on Judaism and Early Christianity.* Atlanta: Scholars Press, 1987.

Breck, John. *The Shape of Biblical Language.* Crestwood, New York: St. Vladimir's Seminary Press, 1994.

Brongers, H. A. "The Literature of the Old Testament." In *The World of the Old Testament,* edited by A. S. van der Woude, 97–164. Grand Rapids: Eerdmans, 1989.

Brodie, Thomas L. *The Gospel According to John: A Literary and Theological Commentary.* New York: Oxford University Press, 1993.

————. *The Quest for the Origins of John's Gospel: A Source-Oriented Approach.* New York: Oxford University Press, 1993.

Bromiley, Geoffrey W. *Theological Dictionary of the New Testament.* Abridged. Grand Rapids: Eerdmans, 1985.

Brown, Raymond E. *The Gospel According to John.* Anchor Bible 29 & 29a. Garden City, New York: Doubleday, 1966, 1970.

————. *The Community of the Beloved Disciple: The Life, Loves, and Hates of an Individual Church in the New Testament Times.* New York: Paulist Press, 1979.

————. "The Relationship to the Fourth Gospel Shared by the Author of I John and by his Opponents." In *Text and Interpretation,* edited by Ernest Best and R. McL. Wilson, 57–68. Cambridge: Cambridge University Press, 1979.

Bultmann, Rudolf. *The Gospel of John: A Commentary.* Philadelphia: Westminster, 1971.

Bunyan, John. *The Pilgrim's Progress.* Westwood, New Jersey: The Christian Library, 1984.

Burge, Gary M. *Interpreting the Gospel of John.* Grand Rapids: Baker, 1992.

Cahill, P. J. "Review of Y Simoens, La Gloire d'aimer," *Catholic Biblical Quarterly* 45 (1983): 709–711.

Campbell, Edward F., Jr. *Ruth.* Anchor Bible 7. Garden City, New York: Doubleday & Company, 1975.

Caird, G. B. *The Language and Imagery of the Bible.* Philadelphia: Westminster, 1980.

Calvin, John. *Commentary on the Gospel according to John,* Vol. 2. Translated by William Pringle. Edinburgh: Calvin Translation Society, 1847.

Carson, D. A. "The Function of the Paraclete in John 16:7–11," *Journal of Biblical Literature* 98 (1979): 547–566.

————. *The Gospel according to John.* Grand Rapids: Eerdmans, 1991.

Cassidy, Richard J. *John's Gospel in New Perspective.* Maryknoll: Orbis, 1992.

Cassuto, Umberto. "The Chiastic Word Pattern in Hebrew," *Catholic Biblical Quarterly* 38: 303–311.

————. "The Function of Chiasmus in Hebrew Poetry," *Catholic Biblical Quarterly* 40: 1–40.

174   *Bibliography*

Cauthron, Halbert A., Jr. *The Meaning of Kingship in Johannine Christology: A Structuralist Exegesis of John 18:1–20:18.* Unpublished Ph.D. dissertation for Vanderbilt University, 1984.

Charlesworth, James H., ed. *The Old Testament Pseudepigrapha,* Vol. 1. Garden City, New York: Doubleday, 1983.

Childs, Brevard S. *Introduction to the Old Testament as Scripture.* Philadelphia: Fortress, 1979.

———. *The New Testament As Canon: An Introduction.* Philadelphia: Fortress, 1984.

Chrysostom, John. "Homilies on the Gospel of St. John," *Nicene and Post-Nicene Fathers.* 1ˢᵗ Series, vol. 14. Grand Rapids: Eerdmans, 1983: 1–334.

Clark, David J. "Criteria for Identifying Chiasm," *Linguistica Biblica* 5 (1975): 63–72.

Coats, George W. *Genesis with an Introduction to Narrative Literature.* Grand Rapids: Eerdmans, 1983.

Collins, Raymond F. *Introduction to the New Testament.* Garden City, New York: Doubleday, 1983.

Cortès, E. *Los discursos de adiós de Gn 49 a Jn 13–17: Pistas para la historia de un génera literario en la intigua literatura judía.* Colectanea San Paciano 23. Barcelona: Herder, 1976.

Cribbs, F. L. "A Reassessment of the Date of Origin and the Destination of the Gospel of John," *Journal of Biblical Literature* 89 (1970): 38–55.

Craigie, Peter C. *Psalm 1–50.* Word Biblical Commentary 19. Waco: Word, 1983.

Culley, R. C. *Oral Formulaic Language in the Biblical Psalms.* Near and Middle Eastern Series 4. Toronto: University Press, 1967.

Cullman, Oscar. *Early Christian Worship.* London: SCM Press, 1953.

———. *The Johannine Circle.* London: SCM Press, 1976.

Culpepper, R. Alan. "The Pivot of John's Prologue," *New Testament Studies* 27 (1981): 1–31.

———. *Anatomy of the Fourth Gospel: A Study in Literary Design.* Philadelphia: Fortress Press, 1983.

———. "The Plot of John's Story of Jesus," *Interpretation* 49 (1995): 347–358.

Dahood, M. J. *Psalms.* Anchor Bible 16. Garden City, New York: Doubleday, 1965.

————. "Chiasmus." In *International Dictionary of the Bible Supplement,* edited by K. Crim, 145. Nashville: Abingdon, 1976.

Davids, Peter H. *Commentary on James.* New International Greek Testament Commentary. Grand Rapids: Eerdmans, 1982.

Deeks, David. "The Structure of the Fourth Gospel," *New Testament Studies* 15 (1969): 107–129.

De Jonge, M. "The Beloved Disciple and the Date of the Gospel of John." In *Text and Interpretation,* edited by Ernest Best and R. McL. Wilson, 99–114. Cambridge: Cambridge University Press, 1979.

Dettwiler, A. *Die Gegenwart des Erhörten: Eine exegetische Studie zu den Johanneischen Abschiedsreden (Joh 13,31–16,33) unter besonderer Berücksichtigung ihres Relecture-Charakters.* Forschungen zur Religion und Literatur des Alten und Neuen Testaments 169. Göttingen: Vandenhoeck & Ruprecht, 1995.

di Marco, A. "Der Chiasmus in der Bibel," *Linguistica Biblica* 36: 21–79, 37: 49–68, 44: 3–70.

Dodd, C. H. *The Interpretation of the Fourth Gospel.* Cambridge: Cambridge University Press, 1953.

duRand, Jan A. *Johannine Perspectives.* Doornfontein, South Africa: Orion, 1991.

Eichrodt, Walther. *Theology of the Old Testament,* Vol. 1. Philadelphia: Westminster, 1961.

Ellis, Peter F. *Matthew: His Mind and his Message.* Collegeville, Minnesota: Liturgical Press, 1974.

————. *Seven Pauline Letters.* Collegeville, Minnesota: Liturgical Press, 1982.

————. *The Genius of John: A composition-critical commentary on the fourth gospel.* Collegeville, Minnesota: Liturgical Press, 1984.

Fee, Gordon D. *The First Epistle to the Corinthians.* Grand Rapids: Eerdmans, 1987.

Fish, Stanley. *Is There a Text in This Class? The Authority of Interpretive Communities.* Cambridge, Massachusetts: Cambridge University Press, 1989.

Fortna, Robert Tomson. *The Fourth Gospel and Its Predecessor: From Narrative Source to Present Gospel.* Philadelphia: Fortress, 1988.

————. *The Gospel of Signs: A Reconstruction of the Narrative Source Underlying the Fourth Gospel.* Cambridge: Cambridge University Press, 1970.

Frederiks, D. C., "Chiasm and Parallel Structure in Qoheleth 5:9–6:9," *Journal of Biblical Literature* 108 (1989): 17–35.

Frye, Northrop. *The Great Code: The Bible and Literature.* New York: Harcourt Brace Jovanovich, 1982.

————. *Words with Power: The Bible and Literature.* New York: Harcourt Brace Jovanovich, 1990.

Gerhard, J. J. *The Literary Unity and the Compositional Method of the Fourth Gospel.* Unpublished doctoral dissertation for Catholic University, Washington, D.C., 1981.

Gerstenberger, Erhard S. "Lyrical Literature." In *The Old Testament and Its Modern Interpreters,* edited by D. A. Knight and G. M. Tucker, 409–444. Philadelphia: Fortress, 1985.

Goldingay, John E. *Daniel.* Word Biblical Commentary 30. Dallas: Word, 1989.

Goppelt, Leonhard. *Typos: The Typological Interpretation of the Old Testament in the New.* Grand Rapids: Eerdmans, 1982.

Grant, Michael. *The Classical Greeks.* New York: Scribners, 1989.

Gundry, Robert H. *Matthew: A Commentary on His Literary and Theological Art.* Grand Rapids: Eerdmans, 1982.

Gunkel, H. *The Legends of Genesis.* Translated by W. H. Carruth. New York: Schocken, 1964.

Guthrie, Donald. *New Testament Introduction.* Downers Grove, Illinois: InterVarsity Press, 1970.

Haenchen, Ernst. *A Commentary on the Gospel of John,* 2 Vols. Philadelphia: Fortress, 1984.

Halpern, Baruch. *The First Historians: The Hebrew Bible and History.* San Francisco: Harper & Row, 1988.

Hamilton, Victor P. *The Book of Genesis: Chapters 1–17.* The New International Commentary on the Old Testament. Grand Rapids: Eerdmans, 1990.

Hanson, Anthony Tyrrell. *The Prophetic Gospel: A Study of John and the Old Testament.* Edinburgh: T & T Clark, 1991.

Harrison, Everett F. *Introduction to the New Testament.* Grand Rapids: Eerdmans, 1971.

Hendriksen, William. *New Testament Commentary: Exposition of the Gospel According to John.* Grand Rapids: Baker, 1953, 1954.

Hengel, Martin. *Judaism and Hellenism,* 2 Vol. Translated by John Bowden. Philadelphia: Fortress Press, 1974.

Hibbert, Giles. *John.* London: Sheed and Ward, 1972.

Hoftizer, J. "Hebrew and Aramaic as Biblical Languages." In *The World of the Bible,* edited by A. S. Van Der Woude, 121–142. Grand Rapids: Eerdmans, 1986.

Horner, Philip B. *Relation Analysis of the Fourth Gospel: A Study in Reader-Response Criticism.* Lewiston, New York: Mellen Biblical Press, 1993.

Howard-Brook, Wes. *Becoming Children of God: John's Gospel and Radical Discipleship.* Maryknoll, New York: Orbis, 1994.

Hultgren, A. J. "The Johannine Footwashing (13:1–11): A Symbol of Eschatological Hospitality," *New Testament Studies* 28 (1982): 539–546.

Iser, Wolfgang. *The Act of Reading: A Theory of Aesthetic Response.* Baltimore: The Johns Hopkins University Press, 1978.

Jeremias, Joachim. "Chiasmus in den Paulusbriefen," *Zeitschrift für die neutestamentliche Wissenschaft* 49 (1958): 145–156.

————. *The Eucharistic Words of Jesus.* Philadelphia: Fortress, 1966.

————. *Abba: The Prayers of Jesus.* Philadelphia: Fortress, 1978.

Johnson, Alfred M. *Structuralism and Biblical Hermeneutics.* Pittsburgh: Pickwick, 1977.

Johnson, Luke T. *The Writings of the New Testament: An Interpretation.* Philadelphia: Fortress, 1986.

Kaefer, J. P. "Les Discours d'adieu en Jean 13:31–17:26 Rédaction et théologie," *Novum Testamentum* 26 (1984): 253–282.

Käsemann, Ernst. *The Testament of Jesus: A Study of the Gospel of John in the Light of Chapter 17.* London: SCM, 1968.

Kennedy, G. A. *New Testament Interpretation through Rhetorical Criticism.* Chapel Hill, North Carolina: University of North Carolina Press, 1984.

Kilpatrick, G. D. "What John tells us about John." In *Studies in John,* Supplements to *Novum Testamentum* 24 (1970), 75–87. Leiden: E. J. Brill, 1970.

Kingsbury, Jack Dean. *Matthew: Structure, Christology, Kingdom.* Philadelphia: Fortress, 1975.

Klauck, Hans-Josef. "Der Weggang Jesu: Neue Arbeiten zu Joh 13–17," *Biblische Zeitschrift* 40 (1996): 236–250.

Klijn, A. F. J. "Patristic Evidence for Jewish Christian and Aramaic Gospel Tradition." In *Text and Interpretation,* edited by Ernest Best and R. McL. Wilson, 169–178. Cambridge: Cambridge University Press, 1979.

Kline, Meredith G. *The Structure of Biblical Authority.* Grand Rapids: Eerdmans, 1972.

Kort, Wesley A. *"Take, Read": Scripture, Textuality, and Cultural Practice.* University Park, Pennsylvania: Pennsylvania State University Press, 1996.

Kümmel, Werner Georg. *Introduction to the New Testament,* revised. Nashville: Abingdon, 1975.

Kurz, William S. "Luke 22:14–38 and Greco-Roman and Biblical Farewell Addresses," *Journal of Biblical Literature* 104 (1985): 251–68.

————. Review of *Becoming Children of God: John's Gospel and Radical Discipleship* by Wes Howard-Brook, *Theological Studies* 56 (1995): 776–777.

Kysar, Robert. *The Fourth Evangelist and His Gospel: An examination of contemporary scholarship.* Minneapolis: Augsburg Publishing House, 1975.

————. "The Fourth Gospel. A Report on Recent Research," *Aufstieg und Niedergang der römischen Welt* 25 (1985): 2506–2568.

————. *John.* Minneapolis: Augsburg, 1986.

Lamouille, A. "Review of Y. Simoens, La Gloire d'aimer," *Revue Biblique* 89: 627–629.

Lasor, William Sanford, David Allen Hubbard, and Frederic William Bush. *Old Testament Survey: The Message, Form, and Background of the Old Testament.* Grand Rapids: Eerdmans, 1982.

Lausberg, H. *Handbuch der literarischen Rhetorik.* Munich: Universität Durkerpresse, 1960.

Lee, Dorothy A. *The Symbolic Narratives of the Fourth Gospel: The Interplay of Form and Meaning.* Journal for the Study of the New Testament Supplement Series 95. Sheffield: Sheffield Academic Press, 1994.

Lee, Lena. "The Structure of the Book of Joel," *Kerux* 7 (1993): 4–24.

Léon-Dufour, Xavier. "Trois chiasmes johanniques," *New Testament Studies* 7 (1960–1961): 249–255.

Lightfoot, R. H. *St. John's Gospel.* London: Oxford University Press, 1956.

Lindars, Barnabas. *Behind the Fourth Gospel.* London: SPCK, 1971.

————. *The Gospel of John.* London: Oliphants, 1972.

Lund, Nils Wilhelm. "The Presence of Chiasmus in the Old Testament," *American Journal of Semitic Languages and Literature* 46 (1929–1930), 104–126.

————. "The Presence of Chiasmus in the New Testament," *Journal of Religion* 10 (1930): 74–93.

————. "The Influence of Chiasmus upon the Structure of the Gospel," *Anglican Theological Review* 13 (1931): 27–48.

————. "The Influence of Chiasmus upon the Structure of the Gospel according to Matthew," *Anglican Theological Review* 13 (1931): 405–433.

————. "The Literary Structure of Paul's Hymn to Love," *Journal of Biblical Literature* 50 (1931): 266–276.

————. "Chiasmus in the Psalms," *American Journal of Semitic Languages and Literature* 49 (1932–1933): 281–312.

————. "The Literary Structure of the Book of Habakkuk," *Journal of Biblical Literature* 53 (1934): 355–370.

————. *Chiasmus in the New Testament,* reprint. Peabody, Massachusetts: Hendrickson Publishers, 1992.

Lussier, Ernest. *Christ's Farewell Discourse.* New York: Alba House, 1979.

Luter, A. Boyd, and Lee, Michelle V. "Philippians as Chiasmus: Key to the Structure, Unity and Theme Questions," *New Testament Studies* 41 (1995): 89–101.

Macgregor, G. H. C., and A. Q. Morton. *The Structure of the Fourth Gospel.* London: Oliver and Boyd, 1961.

Maier, John and Vincent Tollers, editors. *The Bible in its Literary Milieu.* Grand Rapids: Eerdmans, 1978.

Malatesta, E. "The Literary Structure of John 17," *Biblica* 52 (1971): 190–214.

Marrou, H. I. *A History of Education in Antiquity.* New York: Sheed and Ward, 1956.

Marsh, John. *Saint John.* Harmondsworth, England: Penguin, 1968.

Martin, Ralph P. *Carmen Christi,* revised. Grand Rapids: Eerdmans, 1983.

Marshall, I. Howard, editor. *New Testament Interpretation: Essays on Principles and Methods.* Grand Rapids: Eerdmans, 1977.

Martyn, James Louis. *The Gospel of John in Christian History.* New York: Paulist, 1979.

————. *History & Theology in the Fourth Gospel,* revised and enlarged. Nashville: Abingdon, 1979.

McPolin, James. *John.* Wilmington, Delaware: Michael Glazier, Inc., 1979.

Mendenhall, G. E. "Covenant Forms in Israelite Tradition," *The Biblical Archaeologist* 17 (1954): 50–76.

Menken, M. J. J. *Numerical Literary Techniques in John: The Fourth Evangelist's Use of Numbers of Words and Syllables.* Leiden: E. J. Brill, 1985.

Mlakuzhyil, George. *The Christocentric Literary Structure of the Fourth Gospel.* Rome: Editrice Pontificio Istituto Biblico, 1987.

Möller, H. "Strophenbau der Psalmen," *Zeitschrift für die alttestamentliche Wissenschaft* 50 (1932): 240–256.

Moloney, Francis J. *The Gospel of John.* Collegeville, Minnesota: The Liturgical Press, 1998.

Moore, Stephen D. *Literary Criticism and the Gospels.* New Haven: Yale, 1989.

Morris, Leon. *The Gospel According to John.* Grand Rapids: Eerdmans, 1971.

Morrow, Stanley B. *The Gospel of John: A Reading.* New York: Paulist, 1995.

Morton, A. Q., and J. McLeman. *The Genesis of John.* Edinburgh: Saint Andrew Press, 1980.

Motyer, J. Alec. *The Prophecy of Isaiah.* Downers Grove, Illinois: InterVarsity Press, 1993.

Muller, Richard A. "Sanctification." In *International Standard Bible Encyclopedia,* Vol. 4, edited by Geoffrey W. Bromiley, 321–331. Grand Rapids: Eerdmans, 1988.

Munck, Johannes. "Discours d'adieu dans le Nouveau Testament et dans la littérature biblique." In *Aux sources de la tradition chrétienne: Mélanges offerts à M. Maurice Goguel,* Bibliothèque théologique, 155–170. Neuchâtel and Paris: Delachaux & Niestlé, 1950.

Myers, Jacob M. *The Linguistic and Literary Form of the Book of Ruth.* Leiden: E. J. Brill, 1955.

Newbigin, Lesslie. *The Light Has Come: An Exposition of the Fourth Gospel.* Grand Rapids: Eerdmans, 1982.

Nolland, John. *Luke 9:21–18:34.* Word Biblical Commentary 35b. Dallas: Word, 1993.

Norrman, Ralf. *Samuel Butler and the Meaning of Chiasmus.* London: St. Martin's Press, 1986.

O'Day, Gail R. *Revelation in the Fourth Gospel.* Philadelphia: Fortress, 1986.

————. "Toward a Narrative-Critical Study of John," *Interpretation* 49 (1995): 341–346.

Osborne, Grant R. *The Hermeneutical Spiral.* Downers Grove, Illinois: InterVarsity Press, 1991.

Owanga-Welo, Jean. *The Function and Meaning of the Footwashing in the Johannine Passion Narrative: A Structural Approach.* Unpublished Ph.D. dissertation for Emory University, 1980.

Painter, John. "The Influence of Christian Prophecy on the Johannine Portrayal of the Paraclete and Jesus," *New Testament Studies* 25 (1978): 113–123.

————. "The Farewell Discourses and the History of Johannine Christianity," *New Testament Studies* 27 (1980): 525–543.

————. *The Quest for the Messiah: The History, Literature, and Theology of the Johannine Community,* 2nd edition, revised and enlarged. Nashville: Abingdon, 1993.

Pamment, M. "The Fourth Gospel's Beloved Disciple," *Expository Times* 94 (1983): 363–367.

Patte, Daniel. *What is Structural Exegesis?* Guides to Biblical Scholarship. Philadelphia: Fortress, 1976.

Patte, Daniel and Aline Patte. *Structural Exegesis: From Theory to Practice.* Philadelphia: Fortress, 1978.

Porter, Stanley E. and Jeffrey T. Reed. "Philippians As a Macro-Chiasm and Its Exegetical Significance," *New Testament Studies* 44 (1998): 213–231.

Powell, Mark Allan. *What Is Narrative Criticism?* Minneapolis: Fortress, 1990.

Pryor, John W. *John: Evangelist of the Covenant People.* Downers Grove, Illinois: InterVarsity Press, 1992.

Ricoeur, Paul. *Essays on Biblical Interpretation.* Edited and introduced by L. S. Mudge. Philadelphia: Fortress, 1980.

Ridderbos, Herman. *The Gospel of John: A Theological Commentary.* Grand Rapids: Eerdmans, 1997.

Ridderbos, Nicholas H. *De Psalmen: Stilistische Verfahren und Aufbau mit besonderer Berucksichtigung von Ps 1–41.* Beihefte zur Zeitschrift für die alttestamentliche Wissenschaft 117. Berlin: de Gruyter, 1972.

182   *Bibliography*

Ridderbos, Nicholas H. and Herbert M. Wolf. "Poetry, Hebrew." In *The International Standard Bible Encyclopedia* 3, edited by Geoffrey W. Bromiley, 891–898. Grand Rapids: Eerdmans, 1986.

Robinson, John A. T. *The Priority of John.* London: SCM Press, 1985.

Ruppert, L. "Psalm 25 und die Grenze Kultorientierter Psalmenexegese," *Zeitschrift für die alttestamentliche Wissenschaft* 84 (1972): 576–582.

Sanders, James A. *Canon and Community: A Guide to Canonical Criticism.* Philadelphia: Fortress, 1984.

Sanders, J. N. and Mastin, B. A. *A Commentary on the Gospel according to St. John.* New York: Harper & Row, 1968.

Schnackenburg, Rudolf. *Ihr werdet mich sehen: Die Abschiedsworte Jesu nach Joh 13–17.* Freiburg/Basel/Vienna: Herder, 1985.

———. *The Gospel according to St John,* 3 Vols. New York: Crossroad, 1987.

Schneider, Johannes. *Das Evangelium nach Johannes.* Berlin: Evangelische Verlagsanstalt, 1976.

Schnelle, Udo. "Die Abschiedsreden im Johannesevangelium," *Zeitschrift für die neutestamentliche Wissenschaft* 80 (1989): 64–79.

Scott, M. Philip. "Chiastic Structure: A Key to the Interpretation of Mark's Gospel," *Biblical Theology Bulletin* 15 (1985): 17–26.

Segovia, Fernando F. "The Theology and Provenance of John 15:1–17," *Journal of Biblical Literature* 101 (1982): 115–128.

———. "The Structure, *Tendenz,* and *Sitz im Leben* of John 13:31–14:31," *Journal of Biblical Studies* 104 (1985): 471–493.

———. *The Farewell of the Word.* Minneapolis: Fortress, 1991.

SEMEIA 53 (1991) *The Fourth Gospel from a Literary Perspective.*

Simoens, Yves. *La Gloire d'aimer: Structures stylistiques et interprétatives dans le Discours de la Cène (Jn 13–17).* Analecta Biblica 90. Rome: Biblical Institute 1981.

Sloyan, Gerard. *John.* Atlanta: John Knox, 1988.

———. *What Are They Saying about John?* New York: Paulist Press, 1991.

Smalley, Stephen S. "Keeping up with Recent Studies: XII. St. John's Gospel," *Expository Times* 97 (1985–86): 102–108.

———. *1, 2, 3 John.* Word Biblical Commentary 51. Waco: Word, 1984.

Smelik, E. L. *Het Evangelie naar Johannes: de Weg van het Woord.* Nijkerk, the Netherlands: Uitgeverij G. F. Callenbach N. V., 1965.

Smith, Dwight Moody. *The Composition and Order of the Fourth Gospel: Bultmann's Literary Theory.* New Haven and London: Yale University Press, 1965.

————. *Johannine Christianity: Essays on its setting, sources, and theology.* Columbia, South Carolina: University of South Carolina Press, 1984.

————. *John.* Philadelphia: Fortress, 1976.

————. *The Theology of the Gospel of John.* Cambridge: Cambridge University Press, 1995.

Staley, Jeffrey Lloyd. "The Structure of John's Prologue," *Catholic Biblical Quarterly* 48 (1986): 241–64.

————. *The Print's First Kiss: A Rhetorical Investigation of the Implied Reader in the Fourth Gospel.* Atlanta: Scholars Press, 1988.

Sternberg, Meir. *The Poetics of Biblical Narrative.* Bloomington, Indiana: Indiana University Press, 1985.

Stibbe, Mark W. G. *John as Storyteller: Narrative Criticism and the Fourth Gospel.* Cambridge: Cambridge University Press, 1992.

————. *John's Gospel.* London: Routledge, 1994.

Stock, Augustine. "Chiastic Awareness and Education in Antiquity," *Biblical Theology Bulletin* 14 (1984): 23–27.

Talbert, Charles H. *Reading Luke.* New York: Crossroad, 1982.

————. *Reading John.* New York: Crossroad, 1992.

————. "Artistry and Theology: An Analysis of the Architecture of Jn 1,19–5,47," *Catholic Biblical Quarterly* 32 (1970): 341–366.

Tasker, R. V. G. *The Gospel According to St. John.* Grand Rapids: Eerdmans, 1960.

Teeple, Howard M. *The Literary Origin of the Gospel of John.* Evanston, Illinois: Religion and Ethics Institute, Inc., 1974.

Thiering, Barbara. "The Poetic Forms of the Hodayoth," *Journal of Semitic Studies* 8 (1963): 189–209.

Thomas, J. C. *Footwashing in John 13 and the Johannine Community.* Sheffield: JSOT, 1991.

Thomson, Ian H. *Chiasmus in the Pauline Letters.* Sheffield: Sheffield Academic Press, 1995.

Tolmie, D. F. *Jesus' Farewell to the Disciples: John 13:1–17:26 in Narratological Perspective.* Leiden: E. J. Brill, 1995.

Vawter, Bruce. "Ezekiel and John," *Catholic Biblical Quarterly* 26 (1964): 450–458.

Van Leeuwen, Raymond. "What Comes out of God's Mouth," *Catholic Biblical Quarterly* 47 (1985): 55–57.

Van Unnik, W. C. "A Greek Characteristic of Prophecy in the Fourth Gospel." In *Text and Interpretation,* edited by Ernest Best and R. McL. Wilson, 211–230. Cambridge: Cambridge University Press, 1979.

van Ruler, A. A. *Die christliche Kirche und das Alte Testament.* Munich, Germany: Kaiser Verlag, 1955.

Wagner, J. *Auferstehung und Leben. Joh 11,1–12, 19 als Spiegel johanneischer Redaktions- und Theologiegeschichte* Regensburg: Pustet, 1988

Watson, Wilfred. "Further Examples of Semantic-Sonant Chiasmus," *Catholic Biblical Quarterly* 46 (1984): 31–33.

Watts, John D. W. *Isaiah 1–33.* Word Biblical Commentary 24. Waco, Texas: Word, 1985.

—————. *Isaiah 34–66.* Word Biblical Commentary 25. Waco, Texas: Word, 1987.

Wead, David W. *The Literary Devices in John's Gospel.* Basel: Friedrich Reinhardt Kommissionsverlag, 1970.

Webster, E. C. "Pattern in the Fourth Gospel." In *Art and Meaning: Rhetoric in Biblical Literature,* edited by D. J. A. Clines, D. M. Gunn, and A. J. Hauser, 230–257. JSOT Supplement Series #19. Sheffield: JOST, 1982.

Welch, John W. *Chiasmus in Antiquity: Structures, Analyses, Exegesis.* Hildesheim: Gerstenberg, 1981.

Weiss, H. "Footwashing in the Johannine Community," *Novum Testamentum* 21 (1979): 298–325.

Wellhausen J. *Das Evangelium Johannes.* Berlin: Georg Reimer, 1908.

Wenham, Gordon J. *Genesis 1–15.* Word Biblical Commentary 1. Waco: Word, 1987.

Westcott, B. F. *The Gospel According to St. John.* Grand Rapids: Eerdmans, 1954.

Weinfeld, M. "tyrB." In *Theological Dictionary of the Old Testament,* Vol. 2, edited by G. J. Botterweck and Helmer Ringgren, translated by John T. Willis, 253–279. Grand Rapids: Eerdmans, 1975.

White, R. E. O. *The Night He Was Betrayed* Grand Rapids: Eerdmans, 1982.

Wilcox, Max. "On Investigating the Use of the Old Testament in the New Testament." In *Text and Interpretation*, edited by Ernest Best and R. McL. Wilson, 321–244. Cambridge: Cambridge University Press, 1979.

Willis, J. T. "The Juxtaposition of Synonymous and Chiastic Parallelism in Tricola in Old Testament Hebrew Psalm Poetry," *Vetus Testamentum* 29: 465–480.

Winter, Martin. *Das Vermächtnis Jesu und die Abschiedsworte der Vater: Gattungsgeschichtliche Untersuchung der Vermächtnisrede im Blick auf Joh. 13–17.* Forschungen zur Religion und Literatur des Alten und Neuen Testaments 161. Göttingen: Vandenhoeck & Ruprecht, 1994.

Wolfe, K. R. "The Chiastic Structure of Luke-Acts and Some Implications for Worship," *Southwestern Journal of Theology* 22 (1980): 60–71.

Wright, C. J. *Jesus the Revelation of God: His Mission and Message According to St. John.* London: Hodder and Stoughton, 1950.

Wyller, Egil A. "In Solomon's Porch: A Henological Analysis of the Architectonic of the Fourth Gospel," *Studia Theologica* 42 (1988): 151–167.

DATE DUE

DEC 3 0 2003			
DEC 1 5 2008			
MAR 3 1 2015			
			Printed in USA